# RECENT CHANGES
## IN
# AMERICAN CONSTITUTIONAL
## THEORY

BY

## JOHN W. BURGESS, Ph.D., J.U.D., LL.D.

EMERITUS PROFESSOR OF POLITICAL SCIENCE AND
CONSTITUTIONAL LAW, COLUMBIA UNIVERSITY

NEW YORK
COLUMBIA UNIVERSITY PRESS

JK
268
.B84
cop.3

PRINTED IN THE UNITED STATES OF AMERICA

## PREFACE

I DESIRE to acquit the Columbia University Press of any responsibility whatsoever, in the publication of this little book, for the statements, opinions and conclusions contained in it.

These are solely and exclusively my own, and the Columbia University Press, in giving them publicity, without censorship, approval or disapproval, has simply discharged the highest duty of a university, namely, to encourage the complete freedom of inquiry and research and to impart its results to the world.

It will be advantageous to the student of this little book to read it in connection with the work by the same author entitled " The Reconciliation of Government and Liberty," published by Charles Scribner's Sons in the year 1915.

THE AUTHOR.

# CONTENTS

# INTRODUCTION

## IS OUR REPUBLIC IN DECLINE?

I PUT my title in the interrogative form, because, with all my apprehensions and in spite of many disturbing evidences, my whole being revolts against the thought that there is any probability that the unhappy fate of the republics of the past is also to be shared by our own. It is with great effort and no joy that I have brought myself to write this little book, and only the conviction that I owe it to my fellow-countrymen, whether or no they be in the mood to exact the debt or pleased with its payment, could have induced me to assume the thankless task. Especially do I feel that I owe it to the more than ten thousand pupils whom I have been privileged to instruct in the evolution of political history and the principles of political science and constitutional law. In fact, it is to them especially, among whom are included many of the most distinguished publicists, educators, jurists and statesmen of our Country, that I address this, maybe, final word from their old teacher. I know only too well

that what I shall write will appear to contain notes of warning and perhaps traces of
depression, and that such plaints from the old
to the young are not agreeable, are even un-
acceptable, but I fully believe that there are not
many of my old pupils who will not regard this
communication to them as sincere and affection-
ate.   They have, indeed, for the most part, paid
very little heed to the advice which I have ven-
tured, without their solicitation, to intrude upon
them, during the great crisis of 1914 to — who
will dare say what year in the calendar, but I
know only too well the social, business, civil and
political pressure under which they have lived and
to which they have been subjected, to upbraid
them for a lack of moral courage.   The social
ostracism, the business boycott, the arbitrary
arrest and internment, and the lawless confiscation
have imposed upon them and upon all in this once
free land a reign of black and sinister terror, too
overbearing and too overwhelming for any but
supermen to face and defy.

I know only too well whereof I speak.   In my
youth, before 1862, I lived in a community frenzied
by secession and rebellion and I found the with-
ering hate and contempt of those among whom
I had grown up, manifested in every form of
obloquy and aversion, far more difficult to confront

than, later, the artillery and musketry of the Confederate soldiery. Many men are brave enough to stand firm before such tests as the latter, but very few before such as the former. And never before in the history of our Country have so few showed themselves as real men under the supreme test. It were best to draw the veil of oblivion over the weakness of character which like a moral contagion afflicts this good land in these later years, except for the menace to our free institutions contained therein. Intolerance of difference of opinion is death to them. Tolerance of such difference is not enough to maintain them. Respect for it is still insufficient to secure their true development. It must be sought, invited and encouraged, for only through the clash of opinion and the attrition of thought can man press onward towards the goal of truth and the perfection of civilization.

# RECENT CHANGES IN AMERICAN CONSTITUTIONAL THEORY

## CHAPTER I

### THE SYSTEM OF GOVERNMENT AND LIBERTY IN THE POLITICAL SCIENCE AND CONSTITUTIONAL LAW OF THE UNITED STATES IN THE YEAR 1898

I SELECT this date because I hold that the Spanish War of that year was the turning point in our political and constitutional history. Down to that date, the movement of that history had been an almost unbroken march in the direction of a more and more perfect individual liberty and immunity against the powers of government, and a more and more complete and efficient organization and oper- ation of the sovereignty back of both government and liberty, limiting the powers of government and defining and guaranteeing individual liberty. From that date to the present the movement has been in the contrary direction, until now there remains hardly an individual immunity against governmental power which may not be set aside by government, at its own will and discretion, with or without reason, as government itself may determine. In a single proposition, the government of the United States is now, in principle, autocratic. Whether and when it may become such in practice now depends entirely upon the discretion of the governmental authorities. Let us now proceed to demonstrate in detail the elements of this proposition.

In the first place, and as a general statement, we must hold in thought that in all political systems which have a constitutional law, and especially in the political system of the United States, there is a political science as well as a constitutional law, and that this political science is a body of principles derived from the genius and historical development of the people subject to the given political system, and is presumed to be, and ought to be, the foundation of its constitutional law, through which it is expressed in the form of authoritative commands and prohibitions. This political science has, however, of itself no authority as law. It is, simply, a body of principles and usages derived from the teachings of political philosophers and publicists, and from the utterances of statesmen and approved by public opinion.

It is not at all easy to enumerate them, and no catalogue of them which I have ever seen has not, in my opinion, excluded some which it ought to have contained and contained some which it ought to have excluded. I shall not myself undertake, in this little book, anything like an exhaustive treatment of this subject, but will only refer to those axioms and customs in our political system which were most generally accepted as constituting the substance of our political science as understood at the close of the last century.

Before all, the most important of these is the doctrine of individual immunity against governmental power, the principle of the widest possible scope for free action on the part of the individual and of strict limitation in behalf of such action upon the powers of government. This was so pronounced a principle of American political science that down to the close of the last century the menace to the American state was rather too much than too little individualism. This manifested itself in two principal ways, namely, in negro slavery and corporational monopoly. As we all know, sovereignty and government were compelled to interfere and to so limit individualism as to prevent one man from enslaving another and one free combination of men from destroying other such free combinations or individuals not in such combinations, in other words, to prevent individualism from degenerating into caste or class privilege, that is to democratize individualism. ℟ The result of such interference by sovereignty and government was, indeed, a truer individualism and a broader, more general immunity of the individual not only against governmental power, but against the feudalizing tendencies of excessive individualism.    After our experiences with negro slavery and the menace contained in too unrestrained corporational privileges, our American political science seemed to have settled down upon the principle that true conservatism and true progress in political development were one and the same thing, and that they might be defined as such a balance of government and individual liberty as would prevent government from tending towards despotism, or liberty towards anarchy.

In order, however, to secure and preserve such a balance, it had from the outset of our independent history been clear, and in the course of that history it became increasingly clearer, that the organization of an authority back of, and commanding over, both government and individual liberty was an absolute necessity, and this general conviction produced the principle that sovereignty could not be an attribute of government in American political science, but of an organization of the state nearer to the people than government. This doctrine has been expressed under the formula that government in the United States of America " is a government of laws not of men." What is meant exactly by this expression is that government in the United States of America is government by men according to law and under the limitations of law and not according to their own discretion. In other words, that in our system individual liberty is not based on the benevolence of government, but on fundamental immunities against governmental power. But how could this second postulate of our political science be realized? I repeat, only by the introduction of a component element into our political science never before contained in the political science of any country, namely, by the permanent organization of a body back of both government and individual liberty, commanding over both, with the sole and exclusive power of conferring upon government the powers which it may lawfully exercise, and of defining and de-limiting the scope and realm cf individual im-munity against governmental power and securing its proper exercise. How this great doctrine, the most fundamental doctrine of our political science, has been worked out in practice is a topic of our constitutional history and law to which I shall return a little further on.

As the third fundamental of our political science, I would cite the doctrine of local self-government. This doctrine involves, first, the principle that the sovereign power back of both general and local government, that is back of all government, the same power which authorizes and delimits all government over against individual liberty, shall distribute the powers of government in detail between general and local government; and shall do so, secondly, on the basis of two most important considerations, the one being the requirement that local government shall have the maximum of powers which it is capable of exercising, and the other that it shall be the recipient of the residuary powers, that is, of such governmental powers as may be assigned or recognized by the sovereign power back of all government, but not *specifically* assigned to either the general or the local government. The reason for this fundamental principle is, of course, to keep all government, so far as possible, under the influence of the people in the exercise of its powers as well as in the derivation of its tenure.

As the fourth chief doctrine of American political science, I would lay down the principle that all governmental mandate and office are a public trust, to be exercised in strictest independence of all personal interests, prejudices or passions, for the maintenance of individual liberty, the preservation of the public order and the promotion of the general welfare.   This is one of the prime points of distinction between American and European political philosophy, which latter has, almost everywhere and at all times, permitted a personal property, in one respect or another, in governmental office or mandate.

As the fifth doctrine of our political science derived from our political history and practice, I would formulate the proposition that the proper boundaries of a sovereign state are those prescribed by physical geography, economic unity and ethnical solidarity, and, in case these elements do not fully coincide, the emphasis is to be placed in the order in which I have recited them.   What is meant by this statement may be best illustrated by the expression of President Lincoln, when the slave-holders claimed under the now so-called principle of " the self-determination of peoples " that they had the right to secede from the United States.   He said, " No, physically speaking, we cannot separate.   We cannot remove our respective sections from each other, nor build an impassable wall between them."   This emphasis laid upon the element of physical geography in the formation of the proper political boundary of an independent country occurs in his first Inaugural Address before Congress.   In his second Annual

Message to that body, President Lincoln returned to this subject, expressing this principle with still greater distinctness. His words were, " A Nation may be said to consist of its territory, its people and its laws. The territory is the only part which is of certain durability. It is of the first importance to duly consider and estimate this ever-enduring part." In Lincoln's political philosophy, thus, the self-determination of peoples unsupported by the conditions of natural physical boundary is secession pure and simple, no matter with what rhetoric it may be presented, and our Civil War cast this doctrine out of our political science completely and forever. The application of it to Europe by the Versailles pact of 1919 is now widely conceded to be one of the chief causes of the present chaos on that unhappy continent. Ever since the Peace of Westphalia, of 1648, breaking up the Holy Roman Empire into petty states without regard to physical geography or economic unity, Europe has been searching for her natural political unities. With the foundation of the German Empire, in 1871, this aim seemed practically fulfilled and from that date to 1914 Continental Europe enjoyed a period of peace, progress and prosperity never before experienced in all her history.

Europe is physically separated into distinct

parts by the Pyrenees, the Vosges and Ardennes, the Alps, the Carpathians and the Balkans. The states of the continent had in 1871 approximately reached these limits as their political boundaries in the main, with the exception of the region south, and immediately north, of the Balkans and the vast Muscovite Empire. Spain covered the most of the Iberian Peninsula separated from the rest of the continent by the Pyrenees. France largely covered the region between the Pyrenees and the Mediterranean on the south, the Atlantic and the Channel on the west and north and the Vosges and Ardennes on the east. Germany extended approximately over the middle district bounded by the Vosges and Ardennes on the west, the North Sea on the north, the Alps on the south and the Carpathians on the east. Italy covered the middle peninsula cut by the Alps from the body of the continent. Austria-Hungary extended approximately from the Carpathians on the north to the Balkans on the south.

The petty state system of the sixteenth and seventeenth centuries had been thus practically overcome, except, as I have said, in the region immediately north and south of the Balkans. The Versailles pact has extended France across the Vosges and driven a Gallic wedge into the region east of that natural boundary, which is a grave menace to the political unity of that region. It has also driven a corridor between East and West Prussia, which is a constant danger to the peace of that section. It has, furthermore, broken up the natural unity of the territory lying between the Carpathians and the Balkans, the old Austro-Hungarian Empire, into four independent states, and thus sown the seeds of constant war in that region, until it shall find its political unity again. And, finally, it has so shattered the political unity of the great region east and northeast of the Carpathians as to make war probably a permanent status there for decades to come.

This return of chaos in Middle and Eastern Europe is the direct result of the doctrine of secession, renounced, denounced and overthrown in American political science nearly sixty years ago, now named " the self-determination of peoples," and arbitrarily applied as a fundamental principle of the political philosophy of Europe, or more exactly of Middle and Eastern Europe, because Western Europe, and especially Great Britain, have demonstrated the falsity, not to say the hypocrisy, of it by refusing its application to themselves.

As I read the requirements of nature and history in the world's political development, and especially in America's political development, they would have suggested to the sages of Versailles that, instead of breaking up the political unities of Europe, which had slowly and painfully formed themselves to correspond approximately with its natural unities, they should have addressed themselves to the task of creating, or helping to create, a political unity south of the Balkans, of strengthening the national and natural bulwarks of Europe against Asia, and of securing the real freedom of the seas. It is well that the United States has not yet subscribed to a doctrine of political science for Europe which it so decidedly and finally rejected for itself. And if these United States of America shall ever approve of it for Europe or any other part of the world, I greatly fear that its reflex influence will be most injurious to ourselves.

Finally, as the sixth fundamental doctrine of the political science of the United States of America, I would cite the wise recommendation of Washington to avoid the entanglements of European politics or of those of any other countries, and the corollary of this doctrine which advises resistance to the interference of Europe or Asia in the politics of the American continents.

Down to the beginning of the present century this has been so firm and pronounced a principle of our political science as hardly to require statement. During the last twenty-five years, however,

there has arisen a criticism of this doctrine upon
the claim that it isolates us from the rest of the
world and restrains us from doing our part in the
world's civilization.  This claim rests upon the
very serious error that world intercourse and world
interchange of the elements of civilization require
*political* interference and intermeddling.  This is
not only false, but it is so false as to be highly
mischievous and harmful.  Outside of this lies the
whole free realm of trade, commerce, science, liter-
ature, art and social relations, things which bring
all parts of the world together in friendly and helpful interchange, while political intermeddling almost always provokes hatred, enmity and war.

There appears to be an effort now on the part
of certain over-grown European Powers to draw
our Country into the position of a guarantor by
force of arms of their unnatural extent and dom-
inance.  It is to be devoutly hoped that there is
enough sound common sense, as well as genuine
Americanism, left among us, to successfully resist
and thoroughly foil this effort and reëstablish in
full force again the doctrines of Washington and
Monroe upon this subject.

The recent confusion of thought upon this whole
matter has been brought about by the exaggeration
of the sphere of government in the advancement
of civilization, while as a matter of fact govern-

ment plays a quite secondary part in the great work. The freedom of individual thought and expression, of individual initiative and invention, and the free interchange of the results of these great spiritual forces, are the powers which make for civilization both local, national and universal, while governmental interference through its orders, commands, directions, limitations, punishments and wars has done much to restrain rather than always to advance the world's true prosperity.

# CHAPTER II

UPON the basis of these fundamental principles of our political philosophy, we had created by the close of the last century a system of constitutional law and liberty, which represented the furthest advance ever made by the world in political civilization.

In the first place, we had worked out a distinction between sovereignty and government, and had organized sovereignty back of both government and liberty with a distinctness, fullness and completeness never before attained in the world's political history. This Sovereign body, which originally framed and established our Constitution, was a National Convention composed of delegates chosen by the Legislatures of the several States, united in the Articles of Confederation of the year 1781, proposing, and Conventions of the people within the several States approving and adopting.

This was, in spite of a certain show of legality, the original revolutionary organization of the Sovereign authority in our present political system. This Sovereign authority not only created and empowered our system of Government and defined and guaranteed our system of Liberty, but it provided a continuing organization of the Sovereign power independent of, and back of, both Government and Liberty, and endowed it with authority to rearrange each, redefine and reëmpower each, and readjust the boundary between them. This continuing Sovereign authority was composed of the Congress of the new Government, each house thereof acting by a two thirds majority, or a National Convention, called by Congress on the request of the Legislatures of two thirds of the States, proposing, and Conventions of the people in three quarters of the States, or the Legislatures of three quarters thereof, ratifying. This continuing Sovereignty has therefore four possible forms of organization, viz., a combination of the National Legislature, Congress, with the Legislatures of the several States of the Union; a combination of Congress with Conventions of the people in said States; a combination of a National Convention of the people of the United States with Conventions of the people in the several States; and finally a combination of such a National Convention with the Legislatures of the said States. From the Sovereign authority of such body, or bodies, were excepted several subjects, all of which exceptions became obsolete in the year 1808, barring one, the equal representation of the States in the Senate of the United States, which remains today and must remain forever unless set aside or changed by revolution, that is, by a process of force instead of law. This is, certainly, a complex, and, in one respect at least, incomplete, organization of the Sovereign power, independent of, and commanding over Government, but it was the most perfect and significant one known to the world at the close of the last century or ever before. It fulfilled, as never before in the world's political history, the requirements of a complete political science in the sphere of constitutional law. Its vulnerable points had not been taken advantage of by designing men, and therefore had not become clearly manifest, until after the beginning of this century. This part of the subject, however, belongs to the history of our constitutional movement after 1900 and will be treated in that connection.

But before leaving this fundamental element in our constitutional law, I must dwell a moment on the consideration that while our present Constitution was originally founded upon a revolutionary act, or a series of revolutionary acts, it does not recognize any revolutionary right to alter or change it as it now stands.  A right of revolution is a right, if it may be called a right at all, which belongs within the domain of political science, but not within that of constitutional law.

The presumption of constitutional law is that the Constitution once framed on the political science right of revolution contains a legal process for all allowable constitutional change.  If, however, in fact it does not contain any such process, or contains only an inadequate process, there is always the danger that the claim of revolutionary right may be revived, and thoughtless men are too prone to confound political science doctrine with constitutional law right and to ignore the far more stringent conditions and the far more flagrant circumstances which alone justify final recourse to the former, and the immensely greater responsibilities which men incur in so acting.

In the second place, our constitutional law as understood at the close of the last century, and as interpreted at that time, contained a broad realm of individual immunity against all governmental power, municipal, State or National.  In a brief survey of this nature it will not be possible to go into much detail upon this part of our subject; but, happily, this is not necessary in demonstrating the great principle which distinguishes our political and constitutional system from that of any other country in the world, or did do so, at any rate, in the year 1900.

Conciseness upon this point will greatly aid distinctness. Primarily, it was, at the close of the last century, a principle of our constitutional law, we might say the adamantine principle, that the individual citizen and person in these United States was exempt from any power or control by the United States Government, except when such power or control was expressly vested by the Constitution of the United States in said Government, or reasonably and necessarily implied in such expressly vested power or control. It would be impossible to find any dissent from this principle on the part of any reputable publicist, statesman or jurist, or in any judicial decision down, at least, to the close of the last century. It is not necessary, therefore, to amplify this point.

Secondly, the Constitution lays express restrictions upon the Government of the United States and also upon the States in the exercise of all powers which it confers upon, or recognizes to, them, and makes express exemption of a broad realm of individual immunity from them. In this essay I shall confine myself to the restrictions and exemptions laid upon the National Government, for the obvious reason that it is in the exaggeration of the larger powers of this Government that we are to find our chief danger.

The realm of individual immunity against governmental power as defined, described and guaranteed by the express provisions of our constitutional law and interpreted by the Supreme Court of the United States at the close of the last century may be treated under three general heads:

(*a*) The immunity of the individual in respect to his property;

(*b*) His immunity in respect to his physical person; and

(*c*) His immunity in respect to his mind, or thought and its expression.

The approach of government to private property is through three main avenues, viz., the definition of private property, the power to tax and take it, and the power to fix procedure for dealing with it.

At the close of the last century our constitutional law upon these points was that the United States Government had no general power to define private property within the States of the Union, except in regard to patents and copyrights, and no power to prevent an individual from acquiring private property in anything except only in another individual. That is, that the United States Government had no power to enter upon a programme of national governmental socialism by narrowing the concept of private property as then lawful, except in the two instances of patents and copyrights.

Further, that the United States Government could take the property of the individual only through the power of taxation or of eminent domain, and that in the exercise of these powers the Government could levy no direct tax, that is, poll, real estate or income tax, except according to numbers, and no other kind of tax, except with uniformity, which latter limitation the Supreme Court of the United States had defined to mean the same rate, on the same article, everywhere, and could levy no tax on exports at all nor take private property for public use without just compensation. And, finally, that the individual was exempt from all unreasonable searches and seizures of his property through the requirement that the warrants for such procedure should issue only " upon probable cause, supported by oath or affirmation, and particularly describing the place to be searched, and the things to be seized."

In the domain of his bodily or physical immunity the Constitution forbade the Government from issuing " any warrants of arrest except upon probable cause, supported by oath or affirmation, and particularly describing the person to be taken "; or, except in case of invasion or rebellion, to suspend the writ of habeas corpus; or to require

excessive bail; or to delay unreasonably the trial
of any person held; or to prosecute for any crime,
the punishment for which being so grievous as the
deprivation of personal liberty, except by way of
grand jury indictment, that is, presentment by
a body of the accused's fellow-citizens, who should
be in no wise connected with the Government; or
to try for any such alleged crime except by way
of the jury process; or to convict except by the
unanimous agreement of such jury, which should
consist of at least twelve of the accused's fellow-
citizens not connected in any manner with the
Government; or to deport the accused for trial
from the State and district in which the crime was
charged to have been committed; or to authorize
a secret trial; or to deprive the accused of counsel;
or to deny to the accused information of the nature
and cause of his arraignment; or to prevent him
from confronting the witnesses against him; or to
refuse him compulsory process for obtaining witnesses in his favor; or to compel him to give testimony in any manner against himself; or to prosecute him a second time for the same alleged offense
after a lawful verdict; or to pass any bill of attainder, that is, a bill authorizing criminal trial
by any body except a regular judicial body; or
to pass any ex post facto law, that is, any law
making any act a crime or misdemeanor as to

persons committing it before the passage of the law. And lastly, under this head, the Constitution, as it was interpreted by the Supreme Judicial power at the beginning of this century, gave the individual complete immunity against criminal legislation by the United States Government, except upon three subjects, viz., treason, counterfeiting the securities and current coin of the United States and offenses against the law of nations, international law; and in its legislation upon the subject of treason, the Constitution gave the individual immunity against the Government in respect to the definition of treason and the testimony necessary to convict for it, by itself defining treason as consisting only " in levying war upon the United States, or in adhering to their enemies, giving them aid and comfort," and forbidding the conviction of any one for treason " except upon the testimony of two witnesses to the same overt act, or on confession in open court," and also forbidding any punishment of treason by " corruption of blood, or forfeiture, except during the life of the person attainted." This language of the Constitution was held to mean by the highest interpreting authority that to be liable for prosecution for treason a person owing allegiance to the United States must have connected himself with an armed force committing, or intending to commit, acts of violence against the United States, or must have, voluntarily, furnished materials to such a force or to the government to which it belonged knowing that they were to be used for such acts or purpose, or must have voluntarily furnished information or advice to such force or government knowing that it was to be so used. As our constitutional law was understood and interpreted by the supreme interpreting authority in our system at the beginning of this century, the individual was constitutionally immune against the power of the United States Government to convict and punish him for treason under any other interpretation of the meaning of the term.

Our statesmen, publicists and jurists of the year 1900 knew well enough that treason is the criminal concept through which government may wrongfully rid itself of its political opponents. They knew that a party and individuals in opposition to the governing party are an absolute necessity to the preservation of liberty. They knew that the governing party or power must not be allowed to silence argument through criminal prosecution, that it must not be allowed to treat peaceable opposition to its policies as disloyalty to the Country, as treason against the state. They knew that it is quite possible and altogether conceivable that the policy and practice of those in possession, at

any moment, of the powers and offices of government may, at times, approach nearer to treason
against the interests and welfare of the Country
than the views of their opponents.  They held, as
the most essential of all our constitutional immunities, that freedom of thought, argument and criticism must never be suppressed by prosecutions for
treason.

But this leads us to the consideration of this
third, and by far the most important division of
our constitutional immunities against governmental power, the immunity which secures the
mental independence and integrity which alone
can lead to the discovery of truth and right.  The
provision of the Constitution upon this subject is
brief, clear and decisive.  It reads:  " Congress
shall make no law respecting an establishment of
religion, or prohibiting the free exercise thereof;
or abridging the freedom of speech or of the press;
or the right of the people peaceably to assemble,
and to petition the Government for a redress of
grievances."  At one fell blow, the framers of
this Article set aside, thus, the philosophy of the
Orient, of Middle Age Europe, and, in some degree,
of Colonial America, in regard to the search for,
and discovery of, truth in the foundation and development of politics, right and law.  Instead of
the theory of revelation of all truth, the whole

truth and nothing but the truth, from above, at a given time, and to a given person or group of persons, who should by virtue thereof rule the earth and its inhabitants, they fixed the principle in our constitutional law that individual thought, free and untrammeled, and the equally free and untrammeled expression of it, are the only real means for the discovery of truth, right and sound policy, and that only through the attrition of such free thought and speech can a consensus of opinion be reached which can furnish the basis for a real republic in politics, law, economy, letters, ethics or religion.

When the Oriental approached the temple or the tabernacle in which the records of revelation were kept he felt that he was treading upon holy ground and he put the shoes from off his feet. Under the principles of our American philosophy, so firmly fixed and formulated as to be incorporated into our constitutional law, when we near the tabernacle of individual reason and the records of its expression we are on no less holy ground. It is to be approached not only respectfully, but reverently, not simply with tolerance, but with veneration, inviting, encouraging, upholding and defending the action and manifestation of this great spiritual force, through which the truth of the universe is revealed, crudely and mingled with error in the beginning, and making, slowly and painfully, its approximations towards perfection, but the only guide of man in his journey to the goal of his destiny. All of the crafty devices and miserable pretexts, subterfuges and tricks of government to get around, limit and nullify this great immunity by alien and sedition laws, anti-propaganda laws, exaggerated libel and slander laws, anti-contempt laws and the like should meet with stern rebuke from a free people, as should also the still more contemptible methods of social ostracism and business boycott against it. No man who does not recognize the complete freedom of individual thought and expression, antidoted only by the like freedom in every other individual, uncontrolled by government or social or economic repression, as the fundamental principle of American political philosophy, possesses the most essential qualification for citizenship of this republic or any other real republic. He belongs to the Orient with its doctrine of externally revealed truth to a privileged few, and its resultant stagnation, intolerance, persecutions, slaveries and cruel inhumanities.

In the third place, it was, at the close of the last century, a completely established principle of our constitutional law that the Judicial branch of the Government was supreme over the Legislative and Executive branches whenever the issue was one between the constitutional immunities of the individual and the claimed powers of these latter branches. The language of the Constitution upon this point reads as follows: " The judicial power shall extend to all cases, in law and equity, arising under this Constitution, the laws of the United States, and treaties made, or which shall be made, under their authority," etc. Under this jurisdiction over cases arising under the Constitution, the Supreme Court of the United States, especially during the chieftaincy of Justice Marshall, asserted and established the supremacy of the Court over Congress and the Executive in the defense of the constitutional immunities of the individual against governmental power as the fundamental principle and invincible bulwark of American liberty. Any statute of Congress, and any act, or order of the Executive, in violation of these immunities, was held to be, when so pronounced by this Judicial branch, null and void and dare not be executed against the individual. This was well understood and universally observed constitutional law at the beginning of this century, and it was also equally well understood and observed that it was the highest duty of the Court and of all the Courts in the United States to scrupulously protect these individual immunities guaranteed by the Constitution against all governmental power, and never to allow any exaggeration of governmental power over against them. Without that, the mere pronouncements of the Constitution would be, of course, worthless, and if the Courts should withdraw that protection or the Legislative and Executive branches of the Government should cease to regard it and yield to it, then would American constitutional Civil Liberty be at an end, and Government would become a despotism in principle, and would be hindered only by its own benevolence from being a despotism in practice.

This great principle of our Constitution involves one other wide-reaching immunity on the part of the individual, namely, the immunity against any punishment by the Government for judicially resisting the Government in the defense of any of his constitutional immunities. In such a case the individual could not be considered as resisting the law of the land. He would only be asking the proper constitutional authority to tell him whether the constitutional provision under which he might claim immunity was the law of the land or the governmental statute or ordinance, in his opinion, contradicting it. It would be his duty to respect the governmental order while such judicial investigation was in progress, as it would be the duty of the Government to cease at once the execution of its order when enjoined by the Court, or when such order should be pronounced by the Court to be in violation of the constitutional provision, and to make restitution to the individual for the damage or injury suffered by the violation and to refrain from any attempt to apply its order in any similar case to any other individual.

In the fourth place, it was, at the close of the last century, the universally understood doctrine of our political science, and the well established rule of our constitutional law, that the Government of the United States had no authority to suspend any of the provisions of the Constitution guaranteeing individual immunity against governmental power, or any other provisions, unless expressly authorized to do so by the Constitution itself. Searching the Constitution from beginning to end, we find only one clause bearing upon this point. It reads as follows: " The privilege of the writ of habeas corpus shall not be suspended, unless when in cases of rebellion or invasion the public safety may require it."   In placing its interpretation upon this clause, the Supreme Court of the United States, in the great leading case of Ex parte Milligan, held, in the December term of 1866, " that, in the first place, if in foreign invasion or civil war the courts are actually closed, and it is

impossible to administer criminal justice according
to law, then, on the theatre of active military
operations, where war really prevails, there is a
necessity to furnish a substitute for the civil
authority thus overthrown to preserve the safety
of the army and society; and, as no power is left
but the military, it is allowed to govern by martial
rule until the laws can have their free course.   As
necessity creates the rule, so it limits its duration;
for if this government is continued after the courts
are reinstated, it is a gross usurpation of power.
Martial law can never exist where the courts are
open, and in proper and unobstructed exercise of
their jurisdiction.   It is also confined to the locality of active war.   Because during the late Rebellion it could have been enforced in Virginia, where
the national authority was overturned and the
courts driven out, it does not follow it should
obtain in Indiana, where that authority was never
disputed, and always administered.   And so, in
the case of a foreign invasion, martial law may
become a necessity in one State when in another
it would be mere lawless violence."   This Court,
furthermore, laid it down as constitutional law
in this case, that " the suspension of the writ does
not authorize the arrest of any one, but simply
denies to one arrested the privilege of the writ in
order to obtain his liberty."   This was our con-

stitutional theory in the year 1900, and it may be
stated in a single sentence running thus:  There
are, or then were, no war powers in the Government of the United States over the constitutional
immunities of the individual against governmental
authority, except in case of invasion or rebellion,
and then only on the theatre of military operations where the civil courts are closed or cannot
function.

In the fifth place, it was the well understood
and universally approved and appreciated principle of our constitutional law in the year 1900
that the General Government could exercise only
such authority and power as had been expressly
granted to it by the Constitution or by reasonable
and necessary implication from such express grant,
and that all other governmental authority was
reserved to the States of the Union, limited only
by those immunities of the individual secured by
the Constitution against *all* governmental power,
national or local.  This was necessarily involved
in the principle that in a system of federal government the residuary powers of government must,
in the interest of individual liberty, belong to the
States of the Union, especially so when the territory of the Union is of great extent, or when the inhabitants of its political divisions or component
parts are of different racial majorities.

This principle of our constitutional law has been considered, down at least to the year 1900, so fundamental that the only difference of opinion about it related to a few details as to the extent of this residuary power. No party and nobody of any importance claimed residuary powers for the General Government within the Federal organization. There were strict constructionists and liberal constructionists, but there was no party and nobody who claimed any powers for the General Government not expressly vested in it by the Constitution or derived by reasonable, direct implication from express grants. And not even all the powers granted were regarded as exclusive. Many of them were, down to the beginning of this century at least, treated by all parties and interpreted by the Courts as concurrent with the powers of the States of the Union within each State, and as to the subjects under this class the universally accepted rule of interpretation was that the legislation and ordinances of the General Government superseded and annulled those of the States only when the conflict between them was irreconcilable and in no other way to be settled. The powers granted to the General Government related almost entirely to matters of general and uniform interest to and throughout the whole country, that is, relations with foreign countries, relations between the

States of the Union and between the citizens or inhabitants of different States of the Union, and matters within the several States only in so far as they were of fundamental interest throughout the whole country and required the same rules of action everywhere in the serving and promotion of that interest. The one great power of the General Government within this intra-State sphere was the authority and the duty to prevent any State from depriving any person within its jurisdiction " of life, liberty or property without due process of law," or denying " to any person the equal protection of the laws." Within this limitation, practically the whole domestic life and habits of the people were left exclusively to State regulation, except where *all* regulation was forbidden by the constitutional prohibitions in support of individual immunity against *all* governmental power.

Sixth and lastly, the doctrine of attending to our own affairs and of forbidding and resisting the interference of Europe in the affairs of the American continents, usually termed the Monroe Doctrine, had been, by the close of the last century, so far developed and so positively stated as a fundamental rule of our foreign relations as to amount almost to a claim of super-state control by the United States over all the states of both American continents.

During the entire period of our Civil War, these constitutional principles were held so firmly, that no exception to them was tolerated outside of the immediate theater of military operations, where the civil courts were closed and civil government had disappeared and where there was no power to keep order left except the military. At such time and in such place, temporary military rule, that is unlimited rule, was allowed, with the strict understanding that it was to cease the moment the civil courts could again function.

# CHAPTER III

WE will now address ourselves to the task of sur-
veying the road we have been following since the
Spanish War of 1898. It had been, at that date,
just thirty-three years, a generation, since the
youth of America had had the opportunity for
the enjoyment of military glory and the political
and social advancement attendant thereon. It
had been a like period since the sentimentalism
of America had had a really fine subject upon
which to expend itself. The foreign critic of
American character reads us all wrong when he
makes greed the governing principle of our life,
public or domestic. We are good money-getters,
it is true, but we are very generous also as
spenders and givers. I would say that our most
prominent traits are superficiality, sentimentalism,
extravagance and pugnacity. I acknowledge these
are not the last word in civilization, but there is
nothing mean or groveling about them, and they

contain a promise of future development on higher lines.

There appeared on the stage of American political life, just at that moment, the personality through whom the new generation was to have its fittest expression. He was a young man of high birth and of wealthy parentage, educated in two of the first institutions of learning in the land, Harvard College and the Law School of Columbia University. In the latter, he was my own pupil in the political and public law sciences, one of my favorite pupils, and afterwards one of my most esteemed friends. I valued him very highly, although my estimate of his qualities was not then, and never has been, as unqualified as that entertained by many of my countrymen. In looking over the memoranda of my students, I find that I then characterized him as very intelligent though a little inclined to be superficial, impatient, somewhat conceited, honest, entirely self-reliant, generous-hearted, and abnormally pugnacious. The course of his later life did not change that opinion. I regarded him from the first as a man of destiny, and felt sure that he would, sooner or later, lead the young men of the country into an adventure.

The moment for this came in the year 1898, when from the vantage ground of the Navy Department, in which he was first Assistant Secretary, he took up the cause of freeing Cuba from the unnatural and oppressive domination of the Spanish government. There was hardly anybody, old or young, in the United States who did not sympathize with the purpose. Both sound politics and humanity approved it. Whether it ought or ought not to have been done is not, however, our question in this essay, but *how it was* done, and *how it might have been* done. I am quite sure that it might have been done without war and, therefore, at no sacrifice in life and suffering and at much less expense in money than actually occurred.

It was rumored, at least, that Spain would be willing to withdraw from the West Indies for a moderate money consideration and that President McKinley and the more sober members of his Cabinet were favorably inclined to this method of solving the problem. But the ardent spirit of Roosevelt and his kind had no sympathy with such humdrum, dilly-dallying, unspectacular processes. They won their way against the wiser views of the older statesmen, because they, rather than these, represented the cruder, more vigorous, less considerate purposes of the new generation, now arriving at the helm of State. They did not seem to realize that war meant the expansion of govern-

mental power at the expense of individual liberty
and, if they had understood this, it is doubtful
whether it would have deterred them from the pur-
suit of this bellicose program.

It verily seems a sort of historic necessity that
the restlessness of every generation shall find its
outlet in war, in order to bring its real leaders to
the front and by the general exhaustion of the
masses reconcile these to a new period of rest and
obedience. The Spanish War of 1898 was no exception to this order of events. It fixed the popular attention so sharply on Roosevelt that in less
than four years from its conclusion he was seated
in the chair of the President of the Nation and the
people were settling down quietly and obediently
to his program of " progressive Republicanism,"
realized, in part at least, through the methods of
Roughriderism.

From the year 1900 onward any close observer
of American sentiment, as represented by the generation then arriving in authority and power, could
easily perceive that the martial feeling was gain-
ing ground and the military way of solving questions was becoming more favorably regarded than
the civil way. Nothing could have served better
than did the example and successes of Roosevelt
to draw the enterprising, self-reliant, ambitious
young men of the Nation into that line of thought
and action.

Surrounded as he was by the conservative leaders of the Republican Party, he was obliged to move slowly at first, but as the younger generation of that party came gradually into the position of control over its policies he manifested his true autocratic nature, and impregnated his followers rather with the doctrines of democratic Caesarism than with those forming the original basis of the constitutional Republic.

Three things stand out in especial prominence in his extraordinary career from the point of view of the development to which we are, at this point, giving our attention. One was his unauthorized seizure, in a period of peace between these United States and the South American state of Colombia, of the Panama district belonging to this latter state. The Washington Government had been long negotiating for this territory with the purpose of connecting through it the Pacific Ocean with the Caribbean Sea and the Atlantic Ocean, a great enterprise for advancing the commerce of the world. Mr. Roosevelt's impatient nature could not await the slow course of diplomatic bargaining, and he led his Government into one of the most unqualified and arrogant violations of international law known to the modern history of man. The seizure of the Danish Fleet by Great Britain in 1801, and again in 1807, both times in periods of peace between the two countries, did not equal this act of President Roosevelt in the violent, ex parte rupture of the rights of a friendly state, and of the world, since it robbed this friendly state of a part of its most sacred possession, its territory. It was the crassest sort of recourse to the military method of doing things, when the civil method was the only proper one in the case. Roosevelt always boasted of it as a great feat and did not take much pains to excuse himself under the plea of compelling necessity. It had an unfavorable influence over the spirits of our young, ambitious and adventurous men, who idolized Roosevelt as the prototype of Americanism in all things. It made them restive under the restraints and slow processes of law and diplomacy, and incited their tendencies to the quicker and more brutal methods of militarism. We are not likely to exaggerate the baleful effects of this hasty, overbearing act on the part of the President of the United States in the promotion of disrespect for regular constitutional and legal processes and developments.

Another one of the things of especial significance to the subject now under discussion, the changes in our public law since 1900, was his intermediation between Russia and Japan in bringing about the Peace of Portsmouth. This act on his part has always been regarded as pacifistic and it may have been so intended, even by him, but it has worked out as one of the most disastrous things that has ever occurred to the peace of the world. Roosevelt's influence in these negotiations was thrown rather on the side of Japan and the result gave Japan a footing on the Asiatic continent. It is quite probable that Roosevelt thought in this way to hold Japan back from the development of a policy in the Pacific and across the Pacific, which might be a menace to the United States. If such was his idea, it can now be taken as a very patent evidence of his short-sightedness, not to say ignorance, in world politics.

I was in Europe myself at the time of this Treaty and came into contact with the Foreign Ministers of several of the European states, and I found the opinion unanimous among them that the lodgment of Japan in Northern Asia was bound to result in driving half Asiatic Russia back upon Europe, to the ruin of European civilization and indirectly to the injury of North America. When I returned to the United States I communicated this view to Roosevelt. It seemed both to surprise and disturb him. While, therefore, I do not think he can be rightfully charged with any intention or even consciousness of contributing to such a result, the world now knows, trembling as it is under the menace of what is called Bolshevism, which is nothing more nor less than Asiaticism, that the defeat of Russia's Asiatic policy in 1905 is one of the chief things which has made the world of today militaristic on both sides of the Atlantic and on both sides of the Pacific, and which threatens it with a collapse of all civilization and a return to barbarism.

It was, however, in his radical program of 1912, when Roosevelt undertook to lead the younger generation to the support of his campaign for the presidency for the third time, that he contributed most to the transformation of our constitutional theory. I have no doubt that he was entirely honest in this effort and that he really believed this program to be the expression of the principles of sound and progressive development. To us older men of the Republican Party it appeared, on the other hand, to signify an exaggeration of government, a curtailment of civil liberty, and a long step towards Caesarism. His movement caused the fall of the Republican Party from the leadership in the Government and the accession of the Democratic Party to power, the results of which, from the point of view of the development we are tracing, will be seen with greater and greater clearness as we proceed with it.

The first highly important product of the

Rooseveltian radicalism and the triumph of the so-called Democracy of 1912 was the sixteenth Amendment to the Constitution. In the original Constitution no power was given to the Government more grudgingly, or hedged about more carefully, than the power to tax property or to take it by the so-called right of eminent domain. The limitations upon these powers were regarded as among the most vital immunities of the individual against governmental power. The exact wording in which these powers were conferred by the Constitution upon the Government ran as follows: " The Congress shall have power to lay and collect taxes, duties, imposts, and excises," but " no capitation, or other direct tax shall be laid, unless in proportion to the census or enumeration herein before directed to be taken " ; " all duties, imposts and excises shall be uniform throughout the United States "; " no tax or duty shall be laid on articles exported from any State "; no preference shall be given by any regulation of commerce or revenue to the ports of one State over those of another; nor shall vessels bound to, or from, one State be obliged to enter, clear, or pay duties in another; " all bills for raising revenue shall originate in the House of Representatives," and that the levy and collection of taxes shall be for the sole purpose of " paying the debts and providing for the common defense and general welfare of the United States."

The power to take the property of the individual by the right of eminent domain is not even expressly granted to the Government by the Constitution, but is only to be inferred by the limitation imposed upon it which reads: "No person shall be deprived of property without due process of law, nor shall private property be taken for public use, without just compensation."

It can be fairly said that no effort had been made by the Government down to the last decade of the nineteenth century, to nullify or avoid any of these limitations. The political economists of the more democratic school, however, moved probably by the spectacle of the wide differences in individual wealth which had been produced in what I have termed the corporational era of our economic development, had begun to agitate the question of a scheme of taxation which would make the rich pay more than they did under the horizontal scale, so to speak, which the Constitutional limitations on the Government's taxing power had seemed to require. They brought forward their doctrine of proportional equality in taxation, the doctrine of the ascending scale upon increasing amounts. They said that it was not the same thing for a man worth 10,000 dollars to pay a tax of 100 dollars as for a man worth only 1,000 dollars to pay a tax of 10 dollars; that the latter paid much more in proportion than the former. They then, on the basis of this doctrine of proportional equality, began to grope around for a species of tax best adapted to carry out this view, and finally settled down upon a tax on incomes, the annual product from property or labor. They found, indeed, no grant in the express language of the Constitution to the Government to levy and collect an income tax, but they thought that such a power was implied in the grant to impose duties, imposts and excises. It would certainly have been more natural to have derived the authority from the first words of the clause which read, as we have seen, " Congress shall have power to lay and collect taxes," etc., and many of the economists did so find it; but the first successful effort to translate their doctrine into law was made by a Democratic Administration and Congress, and it will be necessary to the complete appreciation of the motives which caused this Administration and this Congress to pass an income tax measure under the authority granted by the Constitution to Congress to " lay and collect duties, imposts and excises," rather than under the authority " to lay and collect taxes," that we remember three things, namely, first, that, as a

duty, an impost or an excise, the limitation imposed upon the exercise of the power to levy and
collect was simply uniformity throughout the
United States; second, that the limitation imposed
by the Constitution on this power in the case of
a tax, however, was distribution among the States
of the Union in proportion to their respective
populations; and third, that the large majority of
the Democratic members of this Congress hailed
from the States south of the old Mason & Dixon
line.  For some reason or other the South wanted
an income tax and wanted it as subject only to
the limitation of uniformity throughout the United
States.  It soon became clear what that reason
was.  The abolition of slavery at the South and
the development of corporational industry at the
North had made the South poor in comparison
with the North, and the South wanted the North
to make a much larger contribution to the support
of the Government.  This could not be accomplished by the income tax provided it were classed
as a direct tax, since the Constitution required
that all direct taxes should be laid and collected
according to the population of the several States,
that is, the limitation would require that a million
inhabitants in one State having annual incomes
of, let us say, one thousand dollars each should
pay the same gross sum as income tax that a mil-

lion of inhabitants in another State each with incomes of, let us say, two thousand dollars a year would be held to pay. On the other hand, should the income tax be classed as a duty, an impost or an excise, it could be laid and collected under the limitation of uniformity throughout the United States and that was thought to allow the Government to tax incomes above an amount fixed by itself while excusing those below that amount from paying any tax at all. The result of that would be, in the case above referred to, that Government might make only all incomes above one thousand dollars subject to the income tax and practically free the inhabitants of the one State from the tax altogether, while imposing it upon the inhabitants of the other State. Or, in case the constitutional limitation of uniformity should require the taxation of all incomes, however small or large, it was contended that Congress might impose a higher rate upon larger incomes throughout the United States than upon smaller, and, in this way, spare the States where the inhabitants were poorer at the expense of those in which they were richer. The Supreme Court of the United States, the ultimate interpreting power of the Constitution when private rights are involved, had ruled that uniformity means the same rate, on the same thing, everywhere, and the upholders of the

income tax as a duty, an impost or an excise contended that an income of one thousand dollars a
year was a different thing from an income of two
thousand dollars a year; that only all incomes of
one thousand dollars, all of two thousand dollars,
and so on, were the same thing.    Consequently,
the first Democratic Congressional Statute imposing a Federal income tax, the Statute of August
15, 1894, classed the income tax as a duty, an
impost or an excise.    Popularly, the tax was
termed an indirect tax, but there was no such
phrase in the Constitution of the United States.
A tax under the language of that Constitution, as
it stood before the sixteenth Amendment, was
either a direct tax or a duty, an impost or an
excise.

The opponents of this tax, however, branded it
as a direct tax and defended themselves against
its levy and collection by judicial resistance to it.
They claimed that, as a direct tax, it could be
laid and collected only on the principle of distribution among the several States of the Union
according to their respective censuses of inhabitants.    The case is known in our Judicial history
as that of Pollock *vs.* the Farmers' Loan & Trust
Company, decided April 8, and May 20, 1895.
It held that the income tax was, under the Constitution of the United States, a direct tax and

could, therefore, be laid and collected by the Government of the United States only under the limitation of the Constitution requiring its distribution in amount among the several States of the Union according to the number of their inhabitants respectively, and that the Congressional Act of August 15, 1894, was, therefore, null and void.

If then an income tax should ever be laid and collected in any other way than this, it would have to be through a reversal of this decision or by Constitutional Amendment.

Those who favored classifying the income tax as a duty, an excise or an impost began to agitate for such an Amendment.  It took nearly twenty years to bring it about, and it would not have been accomplished then except by the joint effort of the Democrats and the Roosevelt wing of the Republican Party, bringing a Democratic Administration and Congress into power in the year 1912, and so transforming the State Legislatures as to bring a sufficient number of them to vote the proposition of Congress upon the subject into the Constitution.

This Amendment, the sixteenth, does not declare that the income tax is not a direct tax, but simply frees its levy and collection by the Government from the limitation imposed by the Constitution upon the levy and collection of direct taxes, *and it imposes no other limitation*. As I understand the situation, therefore, that part of the decision of the Supreme Court in the case of Pollock *vs*. The Farmers' Loan & Trust Company, which declares the income tax a direct tax, still stands as law of the land, while that part of it which declares that it can be levied and collected only under the limitation of a distribution among the States of the Union according to the number of their inhabitants respectively has been nullified by the Amendment.  Of course, if it is still to be classified as a direct tax, it can not come under the limitation imposed upon the collection of duties, imposts and excises, unless this Amendment or some subsequent one so declares, and this has not been done.

We have, therefore, under this sixteenth Amendment, as I interpret it, an investment of the Government with entirely unlimited power in the levy and collection of the most comprehensive of all taxes, the income tax, the tax which can take, thus unlimited, the entire product of all property and all labor.  There is now nothing in our Constitution, as I understand it, to prevent the Government from exercising completely arbitrary, despotic and discriminating powers over the property of the individual through the levy and collection of this unlimited tax upon incomes, unless the

Supreme Court of the United States should interpret this Amendment entirely differently from both the usual and technical meaning of the language in which it is expressed. It is not to be expected that the Court will do this. It is quite clear to the student of our Judicial history that the Court is receding from its earlier staunch position as the defender of the constitutional immunities of the individual against governmental power and is throwing its influence on the side of increasing, by its interpretations, governmental authority at the expense of these immunities. It, too, has come under the spell of war and socialism. It, too, seems to regard the passing of the Old Freedom as necessary to the attainment of the New Freedom.

There is also another thing, a most important thing, to be considered in this connection, and that is whether the exercise of this arbitrary power to tax incomes in the manner and with the purpose manifested in the most recent measures of Congress may not drive us into an unintended and unexpected socialism. All deep students of political science know that political and governmental organization and civilization revolve around two fundamental principles, namely, individualism and socialism, and that the great problem is to arrive at such a balance between these two principles as will avoid anarchy, the excess of individualism, on the one side, and despotism, the excess of socialism, on the other. All such students, especially all profound students of American political science, also know that there are two kinds of socialism, one which I will term voluntary and the other compulsory, and that these United States of America have solved the socialistic problem of their political and governmental civilization, in the higher instances at least, more upon the basis of voluntary socialism than upon that of compulsory socialism. It is this very fact more than anything else which has enabled us to maintain a larger individualism than any other state in the world, and yet to both preserve the public order and accomplish the legitimate ends of socialism.

What is meant by this statement in the concrete is this: Down to this time practically all the finer institutions of our social civilization, our churches, our universities and colleges, our schools of art, our museums of painting and sculpture, our academies and halls of music, etc., have been created and sustained on the principle of voluntary socialism, that is, by the free gifts of money and labor and the free coöperation of individuals. The men and women of wealth in the country have voluntarily made these contributions in money and effort and under freely organized responsibility. If Government shall now arbitrarily take from them the half of their incomes, under the justification that the sliding scale of rates is necessary to a proportional adjustment of the burden of taxation, or under any other justification, real or fancied, will the Government not have deprived them of the means of doing this great socialistic work voluntarily and also have discouraged them therefrom? Now, what may be the result of this mutation of things? May it not be, will it not be, that we shall either have to go without these higher institutions of social civilization or to have them sustained by Government, and therefore under governmental administration? We cannot go without them if we would avoid a return to barbarism. But if we maintain them in the way last indicated, shall we not have swept aside our healthful, peculiarly American distinction between voluntary socialism and compulsory socialism and have enlarged enormously the sphere of compulsory socialism? And what would this be other than the exaggeration of Government at the expense of liberty? It would be just that, and it would be that at the point most vital to real progress in the development of our civilization. It would result in governmental control of religion, philosophy, science, thought and artistic feeling, the very spheres in which the highest results can never be attained except through complete individual liberty, modified only by voluntary association.

From whatever point of view I contemplate this unlimited power vested by the sixteenth Amendment to the Constitution in the Government to take what it will from whom it will, I cannot otherwise interpret it than as signifying a very long step in advance towards governmental despotism and the extinction of the original constitutional immunity of the individual against governmental power in the realm not only of his property, but also of his culture.

# CHAPTER IV

## CONSTITUTIONAL DEVELOPMENT OR TRANSFORMATION DURING THE PERIOD OF 1914–1918

SUCH were not only the tendencies, but actual advances, towards governmental autocracy at the opening of the year 1914. I say autocracy, let it be remembered, because, as I read political science and constitutional law, any government, no matter how chosen and constituted, is autocratic when there is no regular, legally organized authority back of it, which vests it with its powers and limits it in behalf of individual liberty, and an elective government is little, if any, less dangerous than any other in this respect, and its autocracy is generally more vulgar and brutal.

During that period of the Great War while we were neutral, that is down to April 1917, we maintained the form of our constitutional immunities, though somewhat impaired in their original strength by the sixteenth Amendment, but not the spirit of them. Ignorance, intolerance, anger and hate were rapidly and increasingly manifesting themselves among our own people. Social ostracism and even business boycott were practiced against those of our citizens who wished to have the Country take no belligerent part in the great struggle, and the title of Pacifist had become a reproach.   That psychological state of reckless vengeance, which prepares the mind to regard with indifference established rights and institutions, had, in the spring of 1917, taken firm hold upon the larger number of our people and inspired them for persecution at home as well as for war abroad.

About the same moment there appeared, here, as advisers, representatives from foreign governments, who had no appreciation whatsoever of American constitutionalism, and who, therefore, could not have hesitated to counsel the taking of measures irreconcilable therewith according to any of the existing canons of interpretation.   To anyone comprehending the psychological situation, it could not have been a matter of any great surprise that the Government should have, after becoming belligerent, exercised powers before unknown in our constitutional history.

In the first place, Congress enacted the Statute of May 18, 1917, whereby it authorized and ordained a conscript army for foreign war.   This was the first time in our history that the Government had ever assumed the exercise of such a power. By the Statute of April 22, 1898, Congress had declared that " all able-bodied male citizens of the United States, and persons of foreign birth who shall have declared their intention to become citizens of the United States under and in pursuance of the laws thereof, between the ages of eighteen and forty-five years," should constitute the National forces, and with such exceptions and under such conditions as Congress itself might prescribe should be liable to perform military duty in the service of the United States, and by the Statute of June 3, 1916, that " the Army of the United States shall consist of the Regular Army, the Volunteer Army, the Officers Reserve Corps, the National Guard while in the service of the United States, and such other land forces as are now or may hereafter be authorized by law." It is to be observed, however, that neither of these Statutes of 1898 and 1916 directly and specifically ordained the raising of a conscript army for *foreign* war and, in fact, were never so executed. They declare, in a general way, who shall be held to military service in the United States without distinguishing between service in foreign war and service in defense against invasion or against insurrection. The question of the constitutional power of the Government to organize and employ a conscript army in foreign war came, thus, first to issue under the Selective Draft Act of Congress of May 18, 1917, and the several orders of the President in its execution, and its actual execution on the battlefields of Europe.

It was claimed that the Government was authorized to exercise this entirely unlimited control over the life and personal liberty of its subjects — for under such unlimited supremacy in government the individual can be regarded and classified only as a subject — by the war powers granted to it in the Constitution.

Let us next examine these grants of power as expressed in the language of the Constitution. They read as follows: " Congress shall have power to raise and support armies: to provide and maintain a navy: to make rules for the government and regulation of the land and naval forces: to provide for calling forth the militia to execute the laws of the Union, suppress insurrections and repel invasions: to provide for organizing, arming and disciplining the militia, and for governing such part of them as may be employed in the service of the United States, reserving to the States respectively, the appointment of the officers, and the authority of training the militia according to the discipline prescribed by Congress: to declare war and grant letters of marque and reprisal: and to make all laws which shall be necessary and proper for carrying into execution the foregoing powers. The President shall be commander-in-chief of the army and navy of the United States and of the militia of the several States when called into the service of the United States."

It is clear from this language that the Constitution does recognize and authorize universal military duty and service, under the form of the militia of the States, but does not allow the Government of the United States to employ this arm of the service except in defense against invasion, suppression of insurrection and executing the laws of the Union. The militia of the States cannot be, in other words, required by the United States Government to fight a foreign war.

This is not, however, the whole question. The Constitution authorizes Congress to raise and support armies and apparently leaves Congress at its own discretion in determining how and to what extent, under the single express limitation that no appropriation in support of armies or a navy shall be for a longer period than two years. Does, now, this grant of power authorize Congress to raise and employ a conscript army for, and in, foreign war? or does the reference to the militia of the States mean that the only kind of compulsory military service recognized by the Constitution is

this militia, which can be employed only in repelling invasion, suppressing insurrection and
executing the laws of the Union?   The affirmative
of this latter query was undoubtedly the view
held by the vast majority of our statesmen and
jurists at the beginning of the year 1914.   I think
it can be said that it was their view at the beginning of the year 1917.   The practice of the
Government down to that date appeared certainly
to rest upon that principle.   Our foreign wars had
been fought with volunteer armies, and conscription had been employed only in repelling invasion
and suppressing insurrections.   Moreover, the
world practice at the time of the formation of
our Constitution sustains this view of the meaning of the clause vesting the power to raise and
support armies in Congress.   At that time there
was not a state in the world which fought its
foreign wars with a conscript army.   All armies
of that day, employed for that purpose, were
volunteer armies.   When, a couple of years after
our Constitution had been in operation, a proposition was laid before the French Convention to
authorize the raising of a conscript army, it was
rejected with practical unanimity as destructive
of individual liberty.   Not until the year 1798,
when France felt the pressure of the alliance of
many Powers against her Revolution, did her legis-

lature adopt the proposition of Jourdan for a conscript army, and even then its purpose was supposed to be defensive; and it was the abuse made of it by Napoleon in the execution of his imperialistic policy which helped to create the discontent in his rear that contributed to his downfall and then caused the abolition of the system. In the light of this attitude of the world towards a conscript army at the time of the formation of our Constitution, I cannot understand how any fair mind could or can conclude that the framers of that great instrument, jealous as they were of governmental authority and zealous as they were in the defense and preservation of individual liberty, could have vested in the Government a power which even the European states of that day regarded as despotic and unallowable. It must be that they intended that the power vested by them in Congress to " raise and support armies " conveyed only the authority to organize and employ volunteer forces in foreign war, and reserved the compulsory service for repelling invasion, suppressing insurrection and executing the laws of the Union internally against any resistance so strong and widespread as to require a military force to cope with it.

From the point of view of the constitutional immunities of the individual against governmental power, this distinction will be seen, with a little reflection, to be most vital.   For while Congress, that is, the Government of the United States, can always, of its own motion, declare a foreign war, it cannot, of itself alone, produce an invasion of the United States or an insurrection within the Country.   It depends upon other wills as to whether these conditions shall or shall not exist. That is, the Government of the United States cannot, of its own motion, and at any time, create the occasion upon which it may exercise the power of conscription, provided such exercise be limited to the purpose of repelling invasion and suppressing insurrection, but it can do so if it may require the compulsory service of its citizens or subjects in foreign war.   Now the power in a government to conscript its citizens or subjects into its military service upon an occasion which it may, of its own motion, at any time, invent and perpetuate amounts to a power to hold the people of the country under permanent military law, that is, to hold them under a law which is not limited by any constitutional immunities protective of the individual against governmental power, namely, the law governing the army, into which they may all be conscripted, which law Congress is authorized by the Constitution itself to construct and ordain without any limitations whatsoever.

In view of these considerations I cannot believe that the framers of our Constitution vested the power in the Government to raise and employ conscript armies for, and in, foreign war. It is the most despotic power which Government can exercise. It can be so exercised, at any moment, and on occasion created by Government itself, as to sweep away every vestige of individual liberty and put the last drop of blood of every man, woman and child in the country at the arbitrary disposal of the Government.

Notwithstanding these grave objections and these seemingly convincing arguments, it has to be conceded that so far as an Act of Congress, sustained by the approval of the Supreme Court of the United States, and actually executed on the largest scale known to our history, can make it so, the power of the United States Government to raise and employ conscript armies for, and in, foreign war is now the constitutional law of this land. Nothing now short of a reversal of that decision by the Supreme Court or constitutional Amendment to the contrary can make it otherwise. Upon this all-comprehending subject the Constitution as the bulwark of individual liberty against the autocracy of Government is gone, entirely gone. The Government may indeed repeal this particular Statute, but so long as it has the power to reënact it, upon an occasion invented by itself, at any time, as in its unlimited power to declare foreign war, there is no further significance in the constitutional immunities of the individual against governmental power in our American system. It is simply self-deception and folly to conceive that they have any real existence.

It seems, thus, quite clear that the constitutional immunities against governmental power, which we supposed we had in the first decade of this century, in respect to personal liberty and the right to property, have been in the second decade swept away. But more than this has happened. Were our Constitution what we supposed it was in the year 1910, there would still be the opportunity and the possibility, through free and full discussion and through widespread propaganda, of making the people deeply conscious of the great change which has befallen them and of rousing in them the determination to deliver themselves from its further effects, should they so desire, or, should they, on the other hand, approve it as, in their conception of sound development, desirable and beneficial, of consciously positing it as the plan of the future and intelligently working out its parts and adjustments. The Constitution, as has already been remarked, contains prohibitions on governmental power reading as follows:

" Congress shall make no law abridging the freedom of speech, or of the press, or the right of the people peaceably to assemble, and to petition the Government for a redress of grievances," " the privilege of the writ of habeas corpus shall not be suspended, unless when, in cases of rebellion or invasion, the public safety may require it." " No bill of attainder or ex post facto law shall be passed."    The interpretation put upon these clauses by the chief exponents of our constitutional law at the close of the last century ran, in the words of one of them, as follows: " Since the Constitution confers, neither expressly nor impliedly, any power upon the General Government to control the subjects of speech and the press, except, possibly, in the provision authorizing Congress to make all needful rules and regulations respecting the territory or other property belonging to the United States, it must be concluded that this immunity against the power of the Government to pass or execute any law abridging the freedom of speech or of the press, is complete within the States of the Union: that is, the General Government has no power to infringe it in the States either by way of censorship or prevention, or by way of punishment for its use or abuse.    Nevertheless Congress did, in the year 1798, pass an Act for the whole United States

that is, for the States as well as the Territories
and the District of Columbia, making the writing,
printing, uttering or publishing any false, scan-
dalous or malicious writing or writings against the
Government of the United States a crime punish-
able with fine and imprisonment, and several persons were tried and convicted under this Act.
This was one of the most unpopular statutes which
Congress ever enacted. It evoked the noted Ken-
tucky and Virginia Resolutions. It was allowed
to expire in 1801 without any attempt to renew
it. In the District of Columbia, in the Territories
and in places within a State of the Union the
jurisdiction over which shall have been ceded by
the said State to the General Government, this
immunity is less complete than in the States. The
General Government is vested by the Constitution
with general, as distinguished from enumerated
powers in the above-mentioned District, Territories and places. The rule of interpretation as
regards such powers is that what is not denied
is granted. The General Government may, therefore, control the expression of opinion within these
parts of the country, in so far as it is not restrained
therefrom by some provision of the Constitution.
The restriction contained in Article I of the
Amendment that ' Congress shall make no law
abridging the freedom of speech or of the press '

is expressed in general language. It is not limited to the States as to the scope of its action. This restriction upon the power of the Government extends also, therefore, to the District, the Territories and any places subject to the exclusive jurisdiction of the General Government. The question, then, is whether in such parts of the country the immunity is total, or, for the reasons just cited, less than total. In seeking the reply to this question, we are warranted in assuming that this restriction could hardly have been intended to prevent the Government of the United States from introducing and administering the law of slander and libel for the protection of individual reputation in these parts. The common law never held the freedom of speech and of the press to be in any measure infringed by this law of slander and libel for the protection of private character. If such power be not conceded to the General Government, then these parts would be without any law of slander and libel, which would be an unendurable situation in a society professing to exist under the reign of law.

It would inevitably lead to the reëstablishment in practice of the duel, self-help, for the maintenance of personal honor and character. The Constitutional restriction can only mean that the General Government shall create no *unusual* law of slander and libel in such parts, but not that it shall have no law of slander and libel at all, as is prohibited to it in the States; and that signifies that in those parts subject to the exclusive jurisdiction of the General Government this Government must follow, in respect to these subjects, the general principles of our jurisprudence as derived from the common law; that is, for example, it shall not make criticism upon itself or upon the public character of the officials, slander or libel, nor undertake, by way of censorship and prevention, to prohibit the utterance or publication of anything.  Again, in regard to the freedom of assembly and petitioning the Government for redress of grievances, the same distinction must be made between the States and those parts of the country subject to the exclusive jurisdiction of the General Government.  Within the States this immunity is practically total.  The General Government can exercise no powers whatever in regard to the assembling of persons within a State, unless the assembling be for a treasonable purpose, simply because the Constitution does not confer upon the General Government any such powers, and the principle of interpretation which must be applied in determining the extent of the powers possessed by the General Government within the States is that what is not granted by the Constitution is denied, is reserved either to the States or the people. On the other hand, the grant of general powers, as distinguished from enumerated powers, to the General Government in those parts of the country not erected into States, must be interpreted upon the principle that what is not denied is granted. This principle of interpretation would allow the General Government to limit this immunity in such parts by laws distinguishing between a peaceable and a riotous assembly, forbidding the latter and permitting only the former. In such parts, therefore, this immunity against the powers of the General Government is not so complete as in the States. From whatever place the petition may come, however, the duty of the Government to receive it and hear its prayer is the same."

The interpretation placed by the Supreme Court of the United States upon the clause of the Constitution prohibiting the suspension of the privilege of the writ of habeas corpus in the famous Milligan case at the close of the Civil War was, as we have already seen, but because of its transcendent importance here repeated, that, " if, in foreign invasion or civil war, the Courts are actually closed and it is impossible to administer criminal justice according to law, then, on the theatre of active military operations, where war actually prevails, there is a necessity to furnish a substitute for the civil authority thus overthrown, to preserve the safety of the army and society, and as no power is left but the military, it is allowed to govern by martial rule until the laws can have their free course. As necessity creates the rule, so it limits its duration; for if this government is continued after the Courts are reinstated it is a gross usurpation of power. Martial law can never exist where the courts are open, and in the proper and unobstructed exercise of their jurisdiction. It is confined to the locality of actual war. Because, during the late Rebellion, it could have been enforced in Virginia, where the National authority was overturned and the Courts driven out, it does not follow that it should obtain in Indiana, where that authority was never disputed, and justice was always administered. And so in the case of a foreign invasion martial rule may become a necessity in one State when in another it would be mere lawless violence." The Court also further declared, in this case, that " the suspension of the writ of habeas corpus does not authorize the arrest of anyone, but simply denies to one arrested the privilege of this writ in order to obtain his liberty." In other words, the Court held, in regard to this point, that the authority granted by the Constitution to the Government to suspend the privilege of the writ of habeas corpus in time of invasion or rebellion, when, in its judgment, the public safety should require it, did not contain, in itself, any power to suspend any of the other constitutional immunities of the individual against governmental power.

Martial law contains two elements. It is a law over civilians administered by military officials and tribunals, and it is a law exempt from all the limitations imposed by the Constitution on governmental power in behalf of the individual. In other words, it is an unlimited despotism of Government. It is conceivable, however, that Government might be exercised over civilians by military officials and tribunals under the constitutional limitations upon governmental power in behalf of individual liberty. And it is also conceivable that government may be exercised over civilians by the ordinary and regular civil organs *without* these constitutional limitations. Both of these elements of martial law are forbidden by the Constitution as understood at the beginning of this century, except in case of invasion or rebellion, on the theatre of the actual conflict.

The exercise of unlimited governmental power by the civil organs is even more fatal to liberty than its exercise by the military organs. It is not so jealously watched, in fact it is hardly recognized as martial law, and it is far more likely to become the permanent or quasi-permanent order of things. It is called the *war power* of the ordinary Government and men generally have a very hazy notion of what that is, of when and how assumed, of where properly exercised, and when and how terminated. The exercise of these same unlimited powers by the military organs is, on the other hand, far more patent to everybody, and far more easily and generally recognized as temporary and exceptional, and its termination far more promptly required. For these reasons the autocracy of a Major-General is far more tolerable than that of a Legislature or a civil Governor, far easier to reconcile with constitutional liberty.

Summing up in fewer words what has been presented with considerable detail, it may be affirmed that, at the beginning of the year 1917, it was the fundamental law of this Country that the Government had no authority to suppress, or suspend for a single moment, the constitutional immunities of the individual against governmental power, except in case of invasion or rebellion, and then only on the actual theatre of the conflict where the Civil Courts were disabled by the presence of the hostile forces from discharging their duties, and only for so long as this situation might continue. If, in the opinion of any citizen of the United States, or of any person subject to the jurisdiction of the Government of the United States, this Government should undertake, by any of its acts or commands, to deprive such citizen or person of the protection of any of his constitutional immunities against governmental power or suppress or suspend their exercise, it was the constitutional right of such citizen or person to offer judicial resistance to such act or command, either by submitting under protest and reservation of rights and then bringing suit against the Government for restitution, and thus invoking judicial decision of the question between the individual and the Government as to his constitutional immunities, or by a passive disobedience of the governmental act or command, and thus exposing himself to suit before the Courts by the Government or to seizure of his property or personal arrest by it, both of which latter measures would also result, at the will of the individual, in proceedings before the regular Courts where he might raise the question between himself and the Government as to his constitutional immunities — the first through a suit instituted by the individual against the Government for the restitution of his property, and the second by means of an application for the writ of habeas corpus, the privileges of which are assured to him by the Constitution, except in case of invasion or rebellion, on the theatre of actual

conflict. It was understood still further to be
our constitutional law, at the beginning of the
year 1917, that the individual, in case the Judicial Tribunal should decide adversely to him in the
question of his constitutional immunities against
governmental power, had the constitutional right,
either singly and alone, or in conjunction with
others united in peaceable assembly, to appeal to
Congress to draft an Amendment to the Constitution and submit it for ratification to the Legislatures of the States or to Conventions of the people
within the States; or to appeal to the Legislatures
of the several States to request Congress to call
a Convention of the United States for the purpose
of drafting such Amendment and submitting it for
ratification to the Legislatures of the States or to
Conventions of the people within the several
States, which Amendment, when so adopted and
ratified, would override and reverse such judicial
decision claimed by the individual to be a denial
of his constitutional rights and immunities. In all
such resistances to the exercise of governmental
power over him, the individual was regarded as
being entirely within the sphere of his constitutional rights, liberties and immunities, and was
so far from being regarded as disloyal to the Country in making such resistances as to be hailed as
a hero, who was willing to spend his time and

money, and even risk his personal liberty and, maybe, his life, in order to present himself before the ultimate Sovereign in our Constitutional system and secure therefrom the final commanding word in regard to his constitutional rights and immunities and those of his fellow countrymen.

Such deeds require intelligence, knowledge, bravery, generosity, strong character and the spirit of self-sacrifice not second to those of the most intrepid of the world's greatest military leaders. They manifest, at times certainly, a greater loyalty to the Constitution and the Country and to true Americanism than the very Government which may have undertaken to violate, by its own unwarranted usurpations, the fundamental principles of American liberty. Sad indeed will be the day for us when governmental intimidation shall have closed the mouths and palsied the efforts of such wise, courageous and patriotic citizens.

The line separating revolutionary from loyal action was drawn, down to 1917, between the advocacy and advancement of any subject whatever according to constitutional methods, on the one hand, and attempts, on the other hand, at its realization by modes and means violative of, contrary to, or unknown to, the Constitution, and not between subjects according to their supposed character. No matter how radical or ultra-conservative, how excessively progressive or how intensely reactionary, how destructive or how harmfully preservative a proposition might appear to this mind or that, or even to those wielding, at any particular time, governmental power, yet, if presented to the regular governmental authorities and tribunals or to the people in their Sovereign organization, according to the means and methods provided by the Constitution itself, it was not regarded as disloyal or unpatriotic, but as the exercise of the most fundamental constitutional right of the citizen, yea, of any and every person subject to the jurisdiction of the United States Government, as a right not simply to be recognized and endured by the governmental authorities, but as a high prerogative, the exercise of which should be welcomed and encouraged, as pointing the way, the only genuine democratic way, to a true development of politics, law and economics. Suppression by governmental power of the freedom of thought, word and writing, exercised in the regular orderly way prescribed by the Constitution, was regarded as death to growth in all truth and knowledge, and attempts to deal with it by any kind of social or economic boycott, or by any other means than by argument and the better reason, were held by all thinking men to be contemptible acts of ignorant, prejudiced and unfair minds."

Now let us see what the legislation of 1917, popularly entitled the " Espionage Act," did towards placing a new interpretation upon our constitutional law concerning individual immunity against governmental power. In order to be entirely clear upon this point it will be helpful to quote verbatim one or two sections of this Act. It reads as follows: " Whoever, when the United States is at war, shall wilfully make or convey any false reports or false statements with intent to interfere with the operations or success of the Military or Naval forces of the United States or to promote the success of its enemies, or shall wilfully make or convey false reports or false statements, or say or do anything except by way of bona fide and not disloyal advice to an investor or investors with intent to obstruct the sale by the United States of bonds or other securities of the United States, or the making of loans by or to the United States, and whoever, when the United States is at war, shall wilfully cause or attempt to cause, or incite or attempt to incite, insubordination, disloyalty, mutiny, or refusal of duty in the Military or Naval forces of the United States, or shall obstruct, or attempt to obstruct, the recruiting or enlistment service of the United States, and whoever, when the United States is at war, shall wilfully utter, print, write, or publish

any disloyal, scurrilous or abusive language about
the form of Government of the United States,
or the Constitution of the United States, or the
Military or Naval forces of the United States, or
the flag of the United States, or the uniform of the
Army or Navy of the United States, or any language intended to bring the form of Government
of the United States, or the Constitution of the
United States, or the Military and Naval forces
of the United States, or the flag of the United
States, or the uniform of the Army or Navy of
the United States, into contempt, scorn, contumely
or disrepute, or shall wilfully utter, print, write
or publish any language intended to incite, pro-
voke or encourage resistance to the United States
or to promote the cause of its enemies, or shall
wilfully display the flag of any foreign enemy, or
shall wilfully by utterance, writing, printing, publication or language spoken, urge or incite or advocate any curtailment of production in this Country of any thing or things, product or products
necessary or essential to the prosecution of the
war in which the United States may be engaged,
with intent by such curtailment to cripple or
hinder the United States in the prosecution of the
war, and whoever shall wilfully advocate, teach,
defend or suggest the doing of any of the acts or
things in this section enumerated, and whoever

shall by word or act support or favor the cause of any country with which the United States is at war or by word or act oppose the cause of the United States therein, shall be punished by a fine of not more than 10,000 dollars or imprisonment for not more than 20 years or both."

" Whoever harbors or conceals any person who, he knows or has reasonable ground to believe or suspect, has committed, or is about to commit, an offense under this title shall be punished by a fine of not more than 10,000 dollars or imprisonment for not more than 2 years or both."

The first thing to be noticed in the phrasing of this new criminal legislation is that the word war is used in designating the time and occasion for its enforcement, not the words invasion or rebellion, as employed in the Constitution to designate the only time and occasion when and upon which any express power is vested by the Constitution in the Government to suspend any of the immunities of the individual against governmental power. This indicates, of course, that the Government claimed the power through the passage of this Act to exercise such authority as is provided therein during foreign war as well as during invasion and rebellion; that is, upon occasions which the Government may at any time, of its own motion, create or invent and perpetuate, in consequence of military operations outside of the Country, and while our own Civil Courts are open and in the unhindered exercise of their functions. And it is a matter of history that the Government both claimed and enforced such authority during the late war prosecuted on foreign soil three thousand miles away, and for two years after the cessation of military operations still held on to it.

Now what were the provisions of this Act and how do they square with the mandates of the Constitution protective of individual immunity against governmental power?   As cited above, this Act made it a crime under a heavy penalty for any person to use any abusive language about the form of Government of the United States or any language intended to bring this form of Government into disrepute.   Suppose, now, a citizen of the country, learned in political science and constitutional law, should come to the conclusion that a Congress of one House, or a Cabinet responsible to Congress, or an Executive for a life term, were all better forms of Government than our present one, and make and publish an argument for an Amendment to the Constitution to effect such a change, could not that argument be fairly considered language calculated to bring the present form into disrepute, and the person using it be accused of intending this result?   What is bringing a thing into disrepute? One of the synonyms of the word according to the best lexicographers is disesteem, and we always attempt to bring a thing into disesteem when we contrast it with something else, which we undertake to induce men to put in its place. It is the only way to effect such a result. Now how can a prosecution and punishment for such an argument be introduced and imposed by a Government deriving its powers from a Constitution which forbids the passage of any " law abridging the freedom of speech or of the press or the right of the people peaceably to assemble and petition the Government for a redress of grievances," and which vests no power in the Government to suspend any constitutional immunity against governmental power, except the privilege of the writ of habeas corpus in time of invasion or rebellion when the public safety may require it? The only conceivable justification of the Government in the exercise of any such power would be to interpret such an argument as treason, for which crime the Government may declare and impose the punishment; but the Constitution itself ordains that treason shall consist " only in the levying of war against the United States, or adhering to the enemies of the United States, giving them aid and comfort." The presentation of an argument, such as the one above supposed or any other, could not be brought by the wildest canons of interpretation under any of these categories. There is no way, or was, at the beginning of the year 1917, no way provided by the Constitution for the Government to suppress any such language or argument or to punish for its use in speech, writing or printing. There can be no question that, at the beginning of the year 1917, such an Act of the Government would have been held by all preceding authoritative interpretation to be in flat contradiction with the Constitution. There has been no change in the Constitution upon this point since that date. The whole question turns, therefor, upon the interpretation placed by the Supreme Court upon this Espionage Act, as it is popularly called. Does this Court regard the Act as compatible with the provisions of the Constitution? I think it must be conceded that it does. I think it is the law of the United States today, in so far as an Act of Congress, approved by the Supreme Court as constitutional, can make it law, that criticism of the form of Government of the United States in time of foreign war is, if so declared by an Act of Congress, a crime subject to a heavy penalty,* and, since the Government may of its own motion, at any time, declare and legally perpetuate a foreign war, that the

* Schaefer vs. U. S. 251 U. S. Reports, pp. 466–493.

right of the citizen in this respect guaranteed by the first Amendment to the Constitution is now practically worthless. It will now require an Amendment to the Constitution to override such an Act thus sustained by the Supreme Court; but since the citizen or individual who should initiate such a movement might, under the Act, be prosecuted and punished as a criminal, such an Amendment could, in such a situation, be effected only through initiation by the Government itself. That is, in a few words, the Government controls the Constitution in this matter and not the Constitution the Government. This is autocracy, not constitutionalism.

This is but *one* of the points in the so-called "Espionage Act" which, when followed through its legal ramifications, twists and turns, lands us finally in governmental despotism. The Act is, however, bristling with them. It left no point uncovered where the freedom of speech and of the press and of assembly to petition for redress of grievances could be employed in opposition to the will of the Government. It is the direct contradiction of what we once held the Constitution to provide and guarantee. If it is law in all its parts whenever the Government declares it to be, then there is no Constitution left to us as a body of limitations on governmental power, and I think an Act of Congress would again make it law in all its parts in the same sense as in the part particularly discussed. I think, also, that besides the Judicial approval which made it, for the moment at least, constitutional, it had the popular approval and that too very strongly. Men talk and write now about going back to the Constitution since the war is over. But the war was not for two years after the cessation of hostilities legally over, and I have heard or read of no way proposed or suggested of going back to the Constitution except by repeal of this and other Acts by Congress itself. We know that this was the way finally employed. I cannot conceive that this is or will be restoring the Constitution. The Constitution can neither be created, amended, suspended or restored by the Government. The Constitution is not a code of procedure. It is, from the only point of view which hinders Government from becoming autocratic, a body of limitations imposed by the Sovereign Authority upon governmental power. If Government can throw these limitations off and on at its own pleasure, — and this it can do provided it can always invent the occasion for such procedure of its own motion, as it can, by a declaration of foreign war, — then, as I have shown before, they do not really exist at all. As I conceive it, the only way to restore the Constitution to what it was on January 1, 1917, is for the Government and the people to recognize that those Congressional acts and Executive orders suspending the constitutional immunities of the individual against governmental power during foreign war were usurpations and to cease in the future to commit such usurpations, and for the Supreme Court of the United States to reverse all its decisions upholding them as constitutional exercises of governmental power and reaffirm its doctrine in the Milligan case, that these immunities can be constitutionally suspended only in case of invasion or rebellion and then only on the immediate theatre of armed conflict, where and when the Civil Courts are closed and nothing remains but military authority to keep order; or for the Sovereign in our system to enact an Amendment to the Constitution declaring such statutes and orders unconstitutional, null and void *ab initio* and forbidding the enactment of any similar ones in the future.

Firmly convinced as I am that these are the only true ways to restore the Constitution to its original, long-continued and only proper place in our political system, yet I have no hope whatever that either of them will ever be followed. So far as I can gauge the opinion of our people, the great mass of them never had, or have now lost, the distinction between Democratic Caesarism and American Constitutionalism, and seem to feel, for they do not think, that an elected Caesar is the same thing as, or may be a better thing than, government under constitutional limitations in behalf of individual rights and immunities.

I draw this conclusion from their attitude on three most vital subjects, namely, the eighteenth and nineteenth Amendments to the Constitution and the persistent adherence of a large body of the people to a political League of Nations. If we contemplate each of these three things from a purely scientific point of view, the trend towards Caesarism will, as I understand political history and political philosophy, immediately appear in each of them.

First, let us scrutinize the constitutional changes involved in the eighteenth Amendment. They are readily seen to be two-fold in their character, both leading in the same direction, namely, to *centralization* of governmental power and *increase* of governmental power in the General Government. What control had been exercised by government, before the adoption of this Amendment, over the manufacture and sale of intoxicants was determined and administered by the States of the Union.[1] This Amendment now vests this power in

[1] Except, of course, in the Territories and the District of Columbia and in other places subject to the exclusive jurisdiction of the General Government.

the United States Government.  So far it signified only a centralization of governmental power.  So far, therefore, it did not signify any *increase* of governmental power over the individual.  What theretofore the States had been able to do over against the freedom of the individual to eat and drink what he would was simply transferred to the General Government.  But the Amendment went still further than this change of a subject from State jurisdiction to the jurisdiction of the General Government.  It forbade outright the manufacture and sale of intoxicants, that is, it lessened the constitutional exemptions of the individual against the powers of the General Government.  This Government can now, under this Amendment, define what intoxicants are and prevent, by force, their manufacture, sale and use.  The original immunity of the individual against the power of the General Government upon this point has been swept away by the Sovereign itself.

In all the discussions preceding the adoption of this Amendment, this point was not so much emphasized as that relating to the readjustment of the federal system of government.  Men did not seem so much impressed by the fact that the individual was to be totally deprived of his right to determine for himself what he would drink as by the fact that the jurisdiction of the States was to be reduced.  Both results, as I have said, make for unlimited government, but the first-mentioned is a direct withdrawal of an individual immunity, while the second is a shifting of jurisdictions.  A number of the States of the Union had already prohibited the manufacture and sale of intoxicating drinks and we had become somewhat accustomed to Government exercising control of the subject.  It did not seem so much, therefore, a deprivation of individual liberty as a centralization of governmental power already exercised.  The moral argument, too, was more stressed than the political or the legal.  The deplorable consequences of the drink habit were painted in colors so vivid as to blind the view to the questions of governmental centralization and individual immunity from governmental power.  To cure an entire Nation of the curse of drunkenness is certainly a tremendous reform.  The only question is whether, in having recourse to political and legal means, we have taken a road which leads to the loss of liberty and of the sense of personal responsibility and to despotic government.  It remains also to be seen whether National prohibition will, in the long run, prove any more effective than State prohibition, and also whether, in relying upon law, we shall neglect the moral influences, which are so much more valuable to the formation of character.

These are considerations, however, rather apart from the subject I am treating. Whatever may be the result of National constitutional prohibition, it is certain that it has narrowed the domain of individual immunity against governmental power and has vested in the National Government a paternalistic function.

The nineteenth Amendment appears, at first view, to be only a political matter, a question of suffrage extension. But it is suffrage extension of a peculiar and extremely important kind. It is not extension to other individuals of the same class, nationality or sex, or to another class of the same nationality or sex, or to another nationality of the same sex, but to another sex of any class or nationality. Also, it must be remarked, that the extension of suffrage to the female sex has a bearing upon the subject of individual immunity against governmental power in these United States far more important than in any other country in the world.

It has been already explained that the necessary socialism for balancing individualism has been, in this Country, voluntary in a much larger degree than compulsory. In Europe it has, on the contrary, been in larger degree compulsory than voluntary. It has also been explained that the compulsory or state socialism of Europe results necessarily in more governmental control and less individual liberty there than where the greater part of the necessary socialistic aims of the state is accomplished by voluntary effort. And, finally, reference must be had to the fact that the great enterprises of voluntary socialism have been carried forward in this Country more by women than by men. It has been preëminently *their* sphere of communal action. They have been, in chief measure, the makers of the home, the builders of the church and the ministrants of charity, while politics and government have been left for the men. In this way, under these influences, and with this general division of function and activity, the wide realm of voluntary socialism has been administered and preserved, and benevolence and beneficence have made law and force unnecessary in many directions.

The very finest thing which the world's civilization has ever reached is this wonderful sphere in these United States of America of free social co-operation for the advancement of education, religion and morality, the care of the sick and needy, the spread of neighborly kindness and helpfulness, and for the upbuilding, thereby, of enlightened character, which dispenses with paternalism in government and makes democracy safe for our own Country. Without this we could never have attained and maintained that system of limited government and individual liberty which has made us a great and happy and relatively contented people. As we have seen, this great system has received shock after shock since we started out upon that path of conquest in 1898, which veered in the direction of imperialism. It would be a very moderate statement to say that it is now trembling in the balance. It would be nearer the mark to suggest, at least, that it is anxiously awaiting what may be its death blow. If the women of the country, in becoming members of the electorate, shall shift their interest from the home, the church, the school, the hospital, the associations of charity, etc., to the political club, the caucus, the convention, the legislature and office, and abandon their supreme work for civilization within the realm of voluntary socialism, making necessary, thus, the substitution of compulsory socialism, state socialism, governmental socialism, for voluntary socialism, then indeed will the American system of limited government and constitutional civil liberty have made its cycle and reached its end. The impulse will, I conceive, be very strong in that direction. It will call for the exercise on the part of women of great deliberation, intelligence and self-restraint for them to regard, and deal with, these newly won rights, privileges

and glories as incidental to their far higher function of chief ministrants of that great domain of
voluntary socialism, whose existence and sound
development alone can protect us from governmental paternalism and uphold the constitutional
immunities of the individual. It will, for in-
stance, require prudence, patience and persistence,
in full measure, to seek, through the slow and
tedious methods of voluntary contributions the
funds for maintaining the institutions of what I
have called voluntary socialism, when the quicker
and less laborious way of legislative appropriation
may be more freely opened by the votes of women.
Whether this latter course will be followed leading to compulsory, that is, governmental socialism,
will depend most largely, if not entirely, upon the
disposition of the newly enfranchised sex. It would
not be fair to pre-judge them, but it is friendly
and patriotic to call their attention to the great
superiority in importance of their old function
over their new one in our Country's civilization,
and to warn them to maintain it in ever increasing
volume and activity and to make their new political power and influence secondary and subservient
to it.

I must confess, however, pessimistic though it
may appear, that I have no great faith that they
will do so. The pressure is so great, so steady

and so all-sided towards the expansion, intensification and centralization of governmental power, that it sweeps everything in its course. Since the recent enjoyment of three years of despotic power the Government of the United States will probably never again be brought back to its relation to the Constitution obtaining in 1898. The hatreds, suspicions and mistrusts, which war engenders not only between countries, but between citizens of the same country, are the ruin of liberty and the breeder of despotism. It is painful to say, but it must in all truth be said, that women harbor these passions more intensely and more generally than men. Beset with such reflections, an old student of history, political science and public law cannot entertain great hope that women will so use their new political rights, privileges and influences as to maintain, much less increase, the domain of individual liberty, by preserving our system of voluntary socialism, or in any other way. It is rather to be expected that one of the results, by far the most ominously important result, of the nineteenth Amendment, will be the gradual loss of interest by women in their old calling as they become absorbed in the activities of the new, and the gradual expansion of state socialism at the cost of the great American system of voluntary socialism, which has been our glory and our safety.

Finally, we are confronted by a disposition among vast numbers of our people, including some of our best people, to subordinate, somehow and in some degree at least, the constitutional independence of our Country to a world association of Nations. Of course this thing cannot be legally effected otherwise than by an Amendment to our present Constitution. This should be kept distinctly in mind from the outset by every citizen of the Country. It cannot be done by a treaty in the ordinary way. A treaty between the United States Government and any foreign Power, or all foreign Powers, cannot change or modify the Constitution of the United States in the slightest particular. There are those in places of power and influence who seem to think it can, but it appears, at this moment, that the greater number do not.

It is an idea, however, which is not without its attractions. It is claimed that the peace and prosperity of the world depend upon it, and vast numbers sincerely believe this claim to be true. It is to be expected that they will seek a constitutional Amendment, if necessary, to realize their purpose, and it is not impossible that they will succeed. If they do, it will be practically inevitable that governmental power in our system will be thereby increased at the expense of individual liberty. This may not appear in the provisions of the Amendment, but in the operation of the world institutions it will become quickly manifest. A things stood in 1920, without any such Amendment, and without any other provision of the Constitution expressly, or by necessary implication, authorizing it, the Executive Branch of the Government was claiming the power to so commit this country to a " covenant " of Nations with supreme governmental machinery that we could not without dishonor fail to stand by his commitment, and this, to the ear of a constitutional lawyer, strange-sounding claim was supported by a vast number of our people of all sorts and callings.

As Commander-in-Chief of the Army and Navy, the Executive has the constitutional power to agree to an armistice or suspension of hostilities on any conditions not conflicting with the Constitution or laws of the Union. The conditions or terms fixed by him or agreed to by him of the armistice are, within these just mentioned limitations, binding upon the Country without the approval or consent of any other part of the Government. He has, likewise, the power to propose or accept the provisions of a Treaty not conflicting with the Constitution, but must have the concurrence of the Senate therewith in order to bind the Country. It is presumed by international

law and usuage that every country knows the
constitutional law of every other country when
entering into contractual relations with it, and it
is not at all necessary that any attention be called
to the provisions of that law in the case.   In the
matter of the League of Nations urged upon us
in 1919–20, the Executive interwove its covenant
with the Treaty of Peace following the armistice,
a Treaty which violated in a number of particu-
lars the so-called fourteen points regarded as the
basis of the armistice, and the Senate rejected the
Treaty, or perhaps it would be more cautious to
say, failed to ratify the Treaty, because the number of its members necessary to such action or
inaction held that the covenant in the Treaty
would place a super-government over the Government of the United States, which could not be
done by the Treaty-making power of the Government, but only by constitutional Amendment, if
then.   It might also have been well said that, as
the other provisions of the proposed Treaty were
in several very important respects in conflict with
the terms of the armistice, and that, as the Country was legally pledged by the Executive to the
terms of the armistice, the Senate was upholding
the honor of the Country in rejecting, or failing
to ratify, the Treaty and would have conspired
to dishonor the Country had it done otherwise.

In spite of all these facts and considerations, there are still, as I have already said, vast numbers of our people who hold that the Country was in honor bound to accept the Treaty of Versailles with tne league covenant as " its heart," because committed to it by the Executive Branch of the Government.  If such is the case when no clause in the Constitution authorizes the formation of any such League, what will happen should an Amendment to this great instrument be adopted expressly warranting it?  Is it not evident that we might be committed to things by the Government's representatives in the League Organization, which would call for participation in foreign wars, during which, according to the precedents established in 1917 and 1918, the Government may suspend the constitutional immunities of the individual against governmental power and take, without limit, the blood and property of our citizens to be expended in enterprises beyond our own National boundaries and interests?  And is it not also evident, that there would be a still louder clamor, and with more show of reason and obligation, that we should be in honor bound to stand by these commitments as our duty to the world, which duty would be, thereby, placed above our duty to our own Country?  It seems to me that it is quite evident, and would be practically certain to follow any such change in our fundamental law.

We hear ringing all around us the fervid exclamation that the period has now closed for our National exclusiveness, and that we must come out of our isolation and take our part in the world's civilization and recognize and fulfill our duties to humanity, and nobody seems to recognize what an affront it is to our own Country to even hint that we have heretofore preserved ourselves in selfish isolation from the world or have ever failed to discharge our duty to humanity. We have always taken our part in the economic, commercial, educational and charitable affairs of the world, and often at the forefront. We have also made ourselves a shining political model to the world in teaching all its nations and people, by example, within our own boundaries, how to make democracy safe for a Continent and over every variety of nationality gathered within it. Our isolation has consisted simply in not interfering with the internal political or governmental affairs of other countries and not allowing them to interfere in ours. This is not isolation in any proper sense of the word. It is simply the recognition of national political independence, and the right of every people to fashion their internal political government in their own way. Nor has this so-called Monroeism ever prevented us from playing our part in the development of international law and international justice. We have been always insisting on this, and the magnificent palace of International Justice standing in the Hague, built by an American citizen, and associated with the great foundation for cultivating international peace, also his gift, gives flat contradiction to all such inconsiderate and frivolous talk about American isolation, and is a shining proof of our altruistic work for humanity. But we are obliged to confess that this senseless chatter seems very popular and impressive and is one of the forces driving us onward towards the overthrow of our National constitutional system.

We have already gone much too far in the assumption of responsibility for the security and conduct of foreign states by making highly extravagant and enormous loans to several of them.

In the first place there is no provision in the Constitution of the United States vesting any express authority in the Government to loan money or credit to foreign Powers, nor any provision from which such authority may be implied, without having recourse to a far-fetched and highly sophistical course of hermeneutics. This is an entirely sufficient consideration to condemn the exercise of any such authority by the Government as a usurpation of power dangerous to the independence and welfare of the taxpayers and also of the whole people, dangerous not only in an economic sense but also from the point of view of individual liberty in all its ramifications.   The reason for this statement is very plain and very simple.   It is human nature for the creditor, especially when vast sums are involved, to endeavor to shield his debtor from attacks which may destroy or weaken his ability to pay, and even to aid him in offensive movements in order to increase that ability.   The sending of good money after bad, or doubtful, money is proverbial, and when once the occasion for so doing is experienced and the process entered on, neither men nor governments calculate closely the amount of good money, or human effort, or even human life, employed and sacrificed for attaining the end sought.

The arrangement effected with Great Britain by the Government of the United States for the payment, in the period of some sixty years, of the loan of some 5,000,000,000 of dollars made by this Government to that Empire, amounts almost to an alliance between these two Great Powers, in which the United States Government may be called upon to assume, and would probably assume, the task of going to the aid of Great Britain in resisting any attack which might threaten seriously to affect the ability of this Empire to meet this vast obligation.   If the United States Government should now make the like arrangement with the Governments of France, Italy, Belgium and the other states of Europe to which it made loans, the United States would become, thereby, quite possibly the guarantor of the Versailles instrument in its most odious provisions, and, it is at least a reasonable surmise, may thereby be called upon, and possibly induced, to participate in wars between these states and other Powers in order to maintain their ability to discharge these debts. Such entanglements will most likely furnish continual occasion for drawing the United States into foreign wars, which may be declared, and entered on, by the Government at its own will and pleasure, with the now fully precedented accompaniment of an indefinite suspension of every element of individual liberty fixed, defined and guaranteed by the Constitution itself.

Had the United States Government, by forgiving every penny of these debts to all of these debtors — for which it had, and still has, just as much constitutional authority as it had to make the loans to them — induced them all to wipe out the entire war debt between themselves and between them and their enemies, it would most likely have secured to itself and the people of this Country more financial profit within the sixty years fixed for payment, through the general revival of intercourse, trade and prosperity, than the whole amount of the debts represented, to say nothing of the restoration of friendship and good-will between all concerned and throughout the world, and would also have removed the most serious source of menace to the success of our endeavor to recover from the destruction of our great sphere of individual liberty through war and its autocratic accompaniments.

# CHAPTER V

A BRIEF re-survey of what has been said with some detail must bring us to the conclusion that we are facing the menace, at least, of a great change in our system of politics, government and liberty, which may be described briefly, as follows: The extinction of the constitutional immunities of the individual against governmental power, the obliteration of the constitutional distinction between Sovereignty and Government and the possible subordination of National sovereignty and independence to a world state. It is not my purpose to enter into any arguments for or against this momentous reversal of all we have heretofore stood for in the world's political civilization. My task is only to set this movement, as clearly as I am able to do, before the eyes of our people, and indicate its divergence from the path which, to 1898, we had followed with great unanimity, success and prosperity.

It means, first, the loss of that all-important distinction between Sovereignty and Government, which has so fundamentally differentiated the constitutional law of the United States from that of every other great state in the world, and has enabled us to have Government without despotism and Liberty without anarchy. It will avail nothing that the organization of the Sovereign power shall remain nominally distinct from that of the Government, if that Sovereignty shall vest in the Government unlimited authority. In doing so it will have practically abdicated its place of supreme control, which, once lost, is never, without revolution, regained. It shows the decided tendency to commit just this destructive act. The sixteenth and eighteenth Amendments are clear evidence to the mind of any unbiased political scientist and constitutional lawyer of this momentous trend. Everywhere we hear the demand for more government. We are made aware on all sides of great impatience with the slower, more considerate methods of our past life. Prompt and drastic remedy for every conceived ill is the order of the day. Force is called for to take the place of education, argument and persuasion. In a word, the spirit of our people has become imperialistic, and imperialism requires unlimited government, sovereign government.

In the second place, it means the loss of our Individual Liberty as a constitutional immunity

against governmental power. Unlimited government may indulge the individual from time to
time, in one place and another, in a large liberty
of thought, expression and action, but this is all
based on the benevolence *of* government and is
not an independent constitutional right of the individual *against* government, granted or recognized by the Sovereign and guaranteed and secured by the Sovereign against governmental
usurpations and encroachments. It may be, at
any moment, anywhere, withdrawn by government, on its own motion, and the individual left
without defense or recourse. In such a system of
liberty by governmental benevolence the individual is a subject pure and simple, not a citizen
under constitutional protection, and not a mem-
ber of the sovereign body which gives government
its authority and imposes upon it limitations.

As has been emphasized in the foregoing pages,
this system of constitutional immunity against
governmental power, defined and delimited by the
Sovereign and protected by the Sovereign,
through independent Judicial authority, is, or
rather has been, the crowning feature of American public law. Nothing else has so distinguished that law from every other system which
the world has ever produced. The right to vote,
the privilege of holding office or mandate, or

eligibility to party management and leadership, are all bagatelles in comparison with it. Out of it has proceeded that great impulse to private initiative, not only in all forms of business and invention, but also in social betterment, advancement in education, and development in law, economy and politics. If it be now made subject to the benevolence or malevolence of government, as the case may be, it may as well be blotted out of existence at once, so that we may know where we stand in regard to this life and death matter to liberty. Both of the great parties in our politics have been culpable, practically equally so, in bringing about this uncertain situation in the relation of Liberty to Government. Each has vied with the other in the enactment of the statutes suspending the constitutional immunities of the individual everywhere in the United States during a period when we were suffering no invasion or rebellion and when there was no armed conflict upon any part of our territory. And neither has proposed any method of " getting back to the Constitution," as it is called, except by a simple repeal of these statutes by Government, leaving thus the precedent in our public law for the continual reënactment of them on occasions, which may at any time, anywhere, be invented again by Government, upon its own unlimited motion.

This is mere sham, mere self-deception or conscious hypocrisy. The only way now out, the only way to preserve our distinction between Sovereignty and Government, and our system of individual constitutional immunity against governmental power and encroachment, is by a constitutional Amendment, drafted by a National Convention of delegates elected solely for that purpose, and ratified by Conventions within the several States composed of delegates elected solely for that purpose, which Amendment shall declare all statutes suspending the constitutional immunities of the individual during foreign war and all Judicial decisions upholding them null and void *ab initio,* forbid their reënactment and require all future constitutional Amendments to originate in National Constitutional Convention and be adopted by Conventions of the people within the States, each such Convention having the relative weight which the population of the State for which it acts shall have to the whole population of the United States.

Lastly, it means that first our National independence and then our National existence would be continually threatened by the edicts of any super-state in which we might have membership. It is easy to see how our National independence would be undermined thereby. Every power accorded the super-state must be withdrawn from the National states, of course. This requires no demonstration. Neither does it require any argument to prove that a state which has become non-sovereign is no longer independent. This is also self-evident.

It requires, on the other hand, a little more explanation for a full comprehension of what its menace would be to our National existence. We are not a Nation in the sense of a unity of race. At the outset we were more nearly so than we have been at any subsequent time in our history. Today we are a vast conglomerate as to race. There is hardly a race in the world not represented among our people. The elements of National unity having most cohesive power in our system are consequently the geographical and the economic. Our ethnic unity is a consensus of opinion, arrived at by the racial varieties upon our territory through a compromise of racial views, habits and traditions. It is, therefore, philosophical rather than physical, and to arrive at it requires the ability on the part of our political philosophers and statesmen to appreciate the points of view of all the races concerned in regard to every public question, and to reach down in their thought to the very foundation principles upon which all race habits, customs and aims are based. This is a severe requirement, it is true. There is nothing rarer than a correct knowledge of race psychology, and it is not too much to say that it does not exist among the leaders of political thought and action in this Country today. Such being the case, should we become members of a world super-sovereignty in a political sense we would unquestionably be drawn into conflicts between races abroad who are represented in our own citizenship, and the foreign questions leading to those conflicts would become internal questions of our own politics. In other words, under the supposed situation, all foreign wars, or at least, most of them, would tend to become internal struggles with us. Our ignorance of the race and national psychology of foreign peoples would inevitably throw us back upon feeling, instead of reason, in dealing with these foreign questions, and feeling leads to partisanship rather than impartiality, and partisanship leads to intolerance and persecution. Under such conditions civil liberty always perishes and government becomes despotic, and despotic government is not national but imperial. National existence under such conditions is impossible. Anarchy or internationalism are the alternatives.

Heretofore we have followed the course of non-interference in the conflicts of foreign states, nations or races, thereby preventing these conflicts from creating disturbances between the different ethnic elements in our own population. Heretofore, all of these elements have felt equally at home in their American citizenship. Heretofore all of them have been equally concerned in holding this Country free and independent of all foreign interference in its domestic affairs. I am afraid this is not so fully true today. We may fairly imagine what the result would be of our becoming bound, in a super-world-state or in a League of Nations, to interfere regularly and continually in the international or inter-race conflicts of the world. Very recently we have been on the point of offending and alienating one or the other of two of the great races, members of which enter so largely into our own ethnic compound, and it would have been almost comic, had it not been so serious, to see the shifts and subterfuges which the parties engaged in the political campaign of 1920 employed to escape this dilemma. It is to be hoped that we shall escape it. If we do not, we shall be bound to have another element of discord in the ethnical compound of our National unity.

It is thus quite clear that we are on the point of breaking with our past in political science and constitutional law, if we have not already done

so; that we are on the point of substituting despotic government at home and imperialism abroad
for our original distinctly American system of
popular sovereignty, limited government, individual immunity, and non-interference abroad. Are
we doing this consciously and intentionally, or are
we stumbling into it ignorantly, or are we being
led into it by the principle of necessary development, or, as some would say, by the Providence
which guides the world? Upon this I can pro-
nounce no judgment and I do not wish to express
any feeling. I have undertaken to make a statement, to trace a historical movement, not to advance an argument or file a plea. I will only say,
if it be the will of Providence, or the course of
necessary development, then nothing that reason-
ing can do will prevent it. If it be the conscious
and intended purpose of our people well thought
out and finally determined on, then the die is cast
and the feeble voices of a few dissentients will
nothing avail; if, however, we are simply wander-
ing aimlessly and blunderingly, then this plain
presentation may point the way to a change of
the course purposelessly followed. But, as has been
already demonstrated, a real change of the course
is not so simple a thing as merely a repeal of
statutes or a cancellation of executive orders.
It means, at least, a decision of the Supreme

Court of the United States pronouncing all such statutes and orders null and void as violations of the Constitution, and since the Supreme Court has recently shown the tendency of casting its lot with the other Departments of the Government for the increase of governmental power instead of with the individual in defense of constitutional immunities against governmental power, it means still more. It signifies that there must be an Amendment to the Constitution sweeping away all such statutes and orders and also the Judicial decisions upholding them, and making their re-enactment, reissue, and reconfirmation by the Courts, impossible. There is, also, another thing necessary to keep the Sovereign power separate from, and supreme over the Government, namely, the prohibition of governmental interference or participation in amending the Constitution.

As the Constitution now stands there are, as already pointed out, four ways to adopt an amendment to it:

1.   The Amendment may be drafted by a Convention, chosen and assembled for that purpose alone, and proposed by it to Conventions in the several States of the Union for ratification, and ratified by these State Conventions, chosen and assembled for that purpose alone, provided the conventions in three-quarters of the States shall vote in the affirmative.

2. The Amendment may be drafted and presented as in the first case, but presented to the Legislatures of the several States, which by vote of those of three fourths of the States may adopt it.

3. Congress, by a two-thirds majority of both Houses may draft an Amendment and propose it to Conventions in the several States, which may be adopted by these Conventions as in the first case.

4. Congress may draft and propose an Amendment as in the third case, but to the Legislatures of the several States, which may adopt it as in the second case.

In everyone of these methods, except the first, Government participates in the process, and in a certain sense also in the first, since Congress is expressly authorized and required, on the application of the Legislatures of two thirds of the States of the Union, to call the National Constitutional Convention together and impliedly authorized to pass the statutes for the election or choice of the delegates thereto.

In order to separate the Sovereign power completely from the Government, and make it supreme over the Government, it will be necessary to abolish by Amendment the last three methods of Amendment cited, and also to deprive Government of all discretion in the participation assigned it in the first method and make its action therein compulsory and mandatory under the Constitution.

Constitutional Amendments are matters of such fundamental and vital importance that they should be drafted and voted on only by men of the highest quality as jurists, publicists and statesmen, men chosen by the original holders of the suffrage and chosen for that purpose primarily and alone. No mixing of the subjects of Amendment with any other subjects, making compromises instead of principles out of them, should be tolerated, and no office-holding or public place-holding interests should be brought into connection with the supreme duties of the delegates to Constitutional Conventions for drafting and adopting constitutional Amendments. If we would get a clear, distinct and reliable verdict of the Sovereign upon such constitutional fundamentals, we must hold them apart from all considerations of a less important character, and certainly apart from all considerations of political interest and ambition on the part of those immediately entrusted with their framing and enactment.

These are the things which must be done in order to restore the Republic and bring it back on to its constitutional foundation. Nothing short of this will do it, and it is rank folly for us to deceive ourselves in thinking that anything else will. What will happen to us, in case we do not go resolutely forward on this line, is also equally clear. It is not necessary to indulge in prophesy, always unsatisfactory to a scientific mind, in order to set this forth. All we have to do is to comprehend our present status and imagine it as permanent and as in process of further development. It means, as I have already stated, governmental autocracy at home, extinction of all individual constitutional immunity against governmental power and constant war and intermeddling abroad. This has been the usual course of development of the great states of history. Shall it be so with us, or shall we get back onto the old foundation? If we decide for the latter, it has been, so far as I can understand it, demonstrated how and how alone this may be accomplished. But whatever we do must be done now, and will be done now, for if we do nothing but drift further in the course in which we now find ourselves, that is a decision for the reversal of the old principles and traditions of our Republic. If we would not have this, we must make an almost superhuman effort to steer our Ship of State out of this mighty current. It remains to be seen whether we wish to do it, and whether we can do it, if we wish.

COLUMBIA UNIVERSITY PRESS

COLUMBIA UNIVERSITY

NEW YORK

———

FOREIGN AGENT

OXFORD UNIVERSITY PRESS

HUMPHREY MILFORD

AMEN HOUSE, LONDON, E. C.